The New Americans
Recent Immigration and American Society

Edited by
Carola Suárez-Orozco and Marcelo Suárez-Orozco

A Series from LFB Scholarly

Making Connections
A Study of Networking among Immigrant Professionals

Ann D. Bagchi

LFB Scholarly Publishing LLC
New York 2001

Library of Congress Cataloging-in-Publication Data

Bagchi, Ann D. (Ann Dalton)
  Making connections : a study of networking among immigrant
professionals / Ann D. Bagchi.
      p. cm. -- (The new Americans)
  Includes bibliographical references and index.
  ISBN 1-931202-17-6 (alk. paper)
  1. Alien labor--United States. 2. Professional
employees--Social networks--United States. I. Title. II. New
Americans (LFB Scholarly Publishing LLC)
  HD8081.A5 B34 2001
  305.53'08691--dc21

                                                                2001002343

ISBN 1-931202-17-6

Printed on acid-free 250-year-life paper.

Manufactured in the United States of America.

Table of Contents

List of Tables

List of Figures

CHAPTER 1

Introduction
Social Networks and Immigrant Professionals

INTRODUCTION

A vast majority of the work on migrant networks, indeed in the field of immigration studies as a whole, has focused on the experiences of Mexicans (both legal and undocumented) to the detriment of a better understanding of other immigrant groups. This imbalance has not, however, gone unnoticed. Massey et al. (1994) drew attention to the disproportionate coverage of Mexican immigration patterns and noted "Far too much research is centered in Mexico which ... may be unrepresentative of broader patterns and trends. Within the field generally, more attention needs to be devoted to other prominent sending countries" (p. 739).

In addition, in his Presidential Address to the Population Association of America (1996), Massey referred to the current era as the "age of extremes" and called for more research on the affluent. The system of stratification Massey described in his address applies to those immigrants entering through employment preferences. Filling in the occupational gaps left by natives, most of these individuals take either very low status, low-skilled jobs or high status, skill-based positions. It is the latter, relatively "privileged" immigrants who require greater scrutiny according to Massey's perspective.

The 1990s saw some increase in research on immigrant professionals, particularly with a renewed interest in using immigrant skills as a criterion of admission. Some authors suggested a need to move towards a points-based system of admission, as exists in Canada and other Western countries, with preference given to professionals (see, for example, Papademetriou and Yale-Loehr, 1996). Additionally, moves toward a more "globalized" economy and the growth in the technology and medical research industries resulted in greater numerical predominance of skilled and highly educated workers in both the immigrant and non-immigrant streams. These trends, along with the relative lack of research into the topic, motivate this study of immigration among professionals entering the United States.

1

In the following chapters I examine immigration in the context of the networks immigrants utilize. Networks serve a variety of functions in the immigration process, including providing information about the destination society, encouraging sponsorship, and facilitating adaptation to the host society through social, economic and psychological support. Structural explanations for socioeconomic phenomena became more predominant in immigration research throughout the 1980s and 1990s. The popularity of the structural perspective stems from its ability to bridge the gap between macro and micro theories (Cheng and Yang, 1998). As a structural concept, the idea of migrant networks offers a "meso" alternative to the prevailing macro and micro theories[1] and suggests a need for further understanding of how such networks operate.

This study offers meaningful insight into the significance of networks to immigrant professionals due both to the relative neglect of skilled immigrants in past research and to the fact that the types of networks immigrants utilize likely differ between socioeconomic classes. The quality of resources skilled professionals bring to the migration decision-making process differ from those of their less-skilled counterparts. For example, in contrast to laborers, skilled workers more frequently utilize formalized and impersonal network ties (e.g., occupational ties and organized business networks) than personal relations (e.g., family and friendship ties) to gain admission to the United States (Findlay and Garrick, 1990; Findlay and Li, 1998).

I, therefore, address the following key questions in an attempt to identify and explain the structure of networks among immigrant professionals:

1) What is a migrant network and what forms of networks exist?
1) Which types of networks do professionals utilize in the immigration process?
1) Which factors influence the availability and use of networks among professionals?
1) Are there changes in the use of networks over time?

---

[1] Neuman (1997) defines a meso-level theory as one which "attempts to link macro and micro levels or to operate at an intermediate level" (p. 48).

1) Are there differences in network usage according to nativity, occupation, sex and other individual characteristics?
1) What adaptive functions do networks serve?
1) How do professionals perceive their own use of networks?

The answers to these questions appear in the chapters that follow, as outlined below.

BACKGROUND
Immigrant Professionals in the United States
Legislative decisions made with respect to immigration to the U.S. reflect the highly contentious and politicized environment surrounding immigrant admission. Attempts on the part of the government to "protect" American citizens from perceived negative social, political and economic consequences of immigration led to restrictions on, or in some cases special allowances for, particular interest groups. The 1952 Immigration and Nationality Act (popularly known as the McCarran-Walter Act) represented the first piece of legislation to specifically impact, and in this case benefit, skilled workers. This law introduced the first system of preference quotas with those for highly trained workers receiving highest priority. In fact, the law set aside fifty percent of the allowable visas for highly skilled immigrants and members of their immediate families (i.e., spouses and children) (Daniels, 1993). Table 1 1 summarizes the major legislative provisions pertaining to the visa preference system.

The years following passage of the 1952 Act (and prior to the next major change in immigration legislation in 1965) saw fluctuations in the percentage of immigrants entering as professional workers among

Table 1-1: Legislation Affecting the Visa Preference System

1952 McCarran-Walter Act: Eastern Hemisphere (170,000 Visas)
  1st Highly skilled immigrants, their spouses and children (50%)
  2nd Parents and unmarried adult children of U.S. citizens (30%)
  3rd Spouses and unmarried children of permanent residents (20%)
  Visas not allocated to the first three categories assigned as follows:
  4th Siblings/married children of citizens their spouses/children (50%)
  5th Non-preference (any remaining)
  Spouses and unmarried minor children of citizens (no limit)

1965 Hart-Cellar Act: Eastern Hemisphere (170,000 Visas)
  1st Unmarried children > 21 years old of U.S. citizens (20%)
  2nd Spouses and unmarried children of permanent residents (20%)
  3rd Professionals/scientists/artists of "exceptional ability" (10%)
  4th Married children > 21 years old of U.S. citizens (10%)
  5th Siblings of U.S. citizens who are > 21 years old (24%)
  6th Workers in occupations for which a labor shortage exists (10%)
  7th Refugees (6%)
  Spouses, unmarried children and parents of citizens (no limit)

1990 Immigration Act: All Countries (675,000 Visas)
Family Sponsored Preferences
  1st Unmarried offspring of U.S. citizens and their children (3.5%)
  2nd Spouses and unmarried offspring of permanent residents (16.9%)
  3rd Married offspring of U.S. citizens (3.5%)
  4th Brothers and sisters (at least 21 years old) of U.S. citizens (9.6%)
  Spouses, children and parents of U.S. citizens and children born
  abroad to permanent residents (no limit but number of entries
  assumed to be 37.6% of all visas)
Employment-Based Preferences
  1st Priority workers (5.9%)
  2nd Professionals holding advanced degrees or aliens of "exceptional
  ability" (5.9%)
  3rd Skilled workers, professionals, needed unskilled workers and
  Chinese Student Protection Act immigrants (5.9%)
  4th Special immigrants (1.5%)
  5th Employment creation/investors (1.5%)
Diversity Immigrants (8.2%)

those reporting an occupation[2]. In 1953, 7.5% of immigrants reporting an occupation entered in the "professional, technical and kindred" class. That value dropped to a low of 5.9% in 1955-56 and attained its maximum value for the period in 1964 at 9.8% (Keely 1971). Despite some decline in the percentage of professionals admitted as immigrants, however, their absolute numbers increased over the same period. In 1959, the United States admitted 23,287 immigrants as "professional, technical or kindred" workers. Although this number dropped in 1960 and then again in 1961, by 1964 it increased to 28,756 (U.S. Department of Justice, 1955-1964). The discriminatory provision of country quotas likely inhibited a greater increase in the immigration of professional workers (Keely, op cit.). More substantial increases in both the percentage and number of immigrants entering as professionals took place after passage of the 1965 Immigration Act.

The 1965 amendments to the Immigration and Nationality Act (also known as the Hart-Cellar Act) somewhat undermined professional migration in that alterations to the visa preference system favored family reunification over immigrant skills. Close relatives of citizens and permanent residents became the primary beneficiaries of visa allocation while legislative changes reassigned visas for skilled workers to two separate categories. Referring again to Table 1-1, we can see that the new system distinguished between professionals or scientists of exceptional ability and those workers whose occupational skills remained in short supply among the native population. The former dropped from first to third priority while the latter fell to the sixth preference category. After these changes took effect, the two work-related categories combined accounted for only 20% of the allocated visas. The Eilberg Act, an outgrowth of the 1965 act, compounded the negative impact on professional workers in that it shifted the burden of

---

[2] The percentage of immigrants failing to report an occupation to the Immigration and Naturalization Service reaches fairly high levels in some years of data collection. In 1995, for example, excluding homemakers, unemployed and retired persons, students and children under the age of 16, 5.94% of the immigrants admitted as permanent residents did not report an occupation (U.S. Department of Justice 1997, Table 20). However, differences exist by category of admission. Those entering as principal beneficiaries under the occupational preferences more frequently report an occupation than either those entering under family preferences or as derivative beneficiaries.

proof of a labor shortage for the sixth preference category from the Department of Labor to U.S. employers (Yochum and Agarwal, 1988).

However, indirectly, the 1965 act proved a boon to professional workers. Although unintended (Reimers, 1983) the passage of the 1965 amendments led to an increase in the number of persons entering the United States from previously excluded (or numerically controlled) areas of Asia. With the abolition of the national origins quotas and the emphasis on family reunification, Asians began to enter the U.S. in increasingly large numbers and many of the new arrivals came from more highly skilled occupational backgrounds (Friedman, 1973).

After 1965, therefore, the networks of professionals became more sharply delineated into two types. Those persons not qualifying through one of the skill-based categories could utilize their contacts with kin already resident in the United States to obtain entry. Based on these legislative changes, the immigration of professionals increased from 28,790 in 1965 to 46,151 just five years later (U.S. Department of Justice, 1965-1970).

In response to the dramatic increase in migration from the "Third World" and the subsequent growth in job competition between immigrant and native professionals, Congress passed several acts intended to target particular occupational groups. The earliest of these occupation-specific acts passed in 1976. The Health Professions Educational Assistance Act, intended to offer protection from competition within the medical profession, restricted foreign medical school graduates from entering the U.S. to practice or train. Two provisions of this act significantly reduced the number of foreign physicians entering the U.S. First, the law removed all health professions (with the exception of dietitians) from the Department of Labor's Schedule A[3] list of secured occupations. This made the certification process more difficult and created a backlog of persons wishing to enter as health care professionals.

Second, legislative changes now required foreign medical school graduates to pass two parts of a qualifying exam given by the National Board of Medical Examiners and to prove their competency in written

---

[3] The schedule lists those occupations known to suffer from an immediate shortage of labor power throughout the United States. The Department of Labor automatically grants labor certification to any individual (who already has a job offer) seeking entry under one of these occupational titles.

and oral English. These requirements particularly impacted foreign-trained doctors from non-English speaking countries in the "Third World." An amendment to this particular act excused three groups of medical professionals from the exam requirements: graduates of U.S. or Canadian medical schools, medical practitioners of world renown, and those alien doctors practicing medicine in the U.S. prior to January 10, 1977 (Yochum and Agarwal, op cit.). These legislative actions led to a substantial decline in the number of labor certification approvals for foreign-trained doctors attempting to enter the U.S., especially between the years 1977 and 1982 (ibid.). The restrictions also led to greater reliance among physicians and other health care workers on family reunification provisions for gaining entry to the U.S.

In later years Congress enacted legislation specific to the nursing profession. However, unlike the situation for physicians, these legislative measures encouraged increased migration of foreign-born nurses due to a consistent shortage of nurses among the native workforce. In the late 1980s, two laws passed which eased term restrictions for certain categories of non-immigrant nurses. An act passed in 1988 provided term extensions for non-immigrant nurses holding H-1 visas, while passage of the Immigration Nursing Relief Act in 1989 allowed certain non-immigrant nurses to qualify for adjustment to permanent resident status and established a new non-immigrant category for the temporary admission of qualified registered nurses. Frequent changes in immigration laws and regulations increase the value of legally savvy contacts in the destination society. Evidence from case studies of Caribbean immigrants confirms that networks substantially aid nurses in obtaining employment; so much so that, in some major receiving areas, particular ethnic groups now dominate the nursing labor supply (Bashi, 1997).

The most recent large-scale immigration act affecting professional workers passed in 1990. Despite the need for more research into the full effects of the 1990 Immigration Act, ample evidence indicates that this law significantly altered the context of professional migration. The INS aptly described the act as a "major overhaul of immigration law" (U.S. Department of Justice, 1997: A.1-20). The law increased total immigration to 675,000 annually beginning in fiscal year (FY) 1995 (up from a total of 270,000 in place since 1980 but reduced from the cap of 700,000 in place during fiscal years 1992-1994). While immediate relatives of U.S. citizens and four other family preference categories accounted for 480,000 of the total visas to be awarded, a new categorization of employment-based admissions added 140,000 visas to the total. The act also reserved 55,000 visas for a newly created category called "diversity immigrants[4]." In addition to these changes in the level of immigration and in the visa preferences, the 1990 Act revised existing non-immigrant admissions criteria and created several new categories.

Within the employment-based visa category, professionals earned a more predominant place under the 1990 Act. Highly trained professionals (those professors, scientists and researchers of "extraordinary ability") receive reservations for 80,000 of the 120,000 visas set aside under the employment-related preferences. Among the 40,000 remaining employment-based visas, no more than 10,000 may go to unskilled workers. At least 30,000 of these visas are specifically set aside for professionals with at least a bachelor's or equivalent degree or other skilled workers (those whose jobs require at least two years of training or experience)[5].

The employment-related provisions came into effect in FY 1992 and resulted in large increases in the immigration of scientists and engineers. According to reports by the National Science Foundation and the National Research Council these legislative changes account for the fact that the number of scientists, engineers and technicians entering the U.S. increased by 3.1% at the same time that total immigration declined by 7.2%. By 1994, professionals accounted for 67,286 (8.36%) of the immigrants admitted, although this value had dropped to 45,088 (6.83% of the total) by 1998.

Although the quotas reserved for highly skilled workers and other professionals likely did account for a considerable part of the increase in immigration among the aforementioned groups, family reunification

---

[4] The introduction of a "diversity immigrants" category reflects an attempt to rectify the "adverse affects" of the 1965 Immigration Act. The unexpected increase in Asian immigration after 1965 coincided with a decrease in immigration from many traditional sending countries in Europe. The introduction of diversity immigrant visas represents Congresses attempt to re-establish immigration from these areas. The law reserves no less than 40% of these visas for natives of Ireland (including Northern Ireland).

[5] Spouses and children of employment-based immigrants enter as dependents of the principal, with their visas counting toward the total for each category.

remained an important source of entry for unprotected professionals, such as physicians. These facts suggest a need to determine the importance of migrant networks in facilitating immigration through familial visa categories. Similarly, it becomes relevant to ask whether family-based (or other informal) networks or job-related (or other formal) networks predominate in these processes.

The research that follows addresses these and other questions regarding the use of networks among immigrant professionals. The analyses focus specifically on the following four occupational groups based on their high percentages of foreign-born workers: nurses, physicians, engineers and scientists. In addition, immigrants from India and the Philippines represent specific case studies in two of the chapters to follow. I chose these countries based on the predominance of these two sending areas within the aforementioned occupations.

Prominent Immigration Theories
The development of international migration theories began with micro-level conceptualizations assessing the costs and benefits of moving from one location to another. According to these push-pull formulations, a typical migrant weighed the factors pushing them out of their source country (e.g., poor wages or working conditions) against the benefits available in a particular destination area (e.g., improved job status and pay) and chose to migrate when the benefits out-weighed the costs. Although social and political factors could also influence individual decision-making, these theories generally focused on the economic factors pertinent in the sending and receiving countries.

Versions of the push-pull models include Todaro's (1976) Expected Income Hypothesis and Stark's (1991) New Economics of Migration model. In Todaro's formulation, an individual considering immigration estimates potential income in the destination country over a specified time horizon and factors in the probability of actually obtaining a job there. The individual then contrasts this value with expected earnings in the home country, taking into account the benefits of money earned in the present time versus possible future earnings. The difference between these values reflects the overall net return to migration and the likelihood of an individual choosing to immigrate. Todaro's model moves beyond a simple cost-benefit analysis of immediate gains and losses but remains focused on individual decision-making and the centrality of economic factors in the migration process.

Stark's New Economics of Migration offers further modification of the classic push-pull framework in that it takes family and household concerns into account in the decision-making process. Stark's emphasis on the role of collectivities such as the family represents the most important break in this line of thinking (Massey et al., 1993). The New Economics of Migration considers migration as part of a family strategy for income maximization. In an attempt to diversify family income generating strategies, some members remain in the local labor market while others take opportunities to earn from abroad. This model applies well to the conditions facing many less skilled workers in developing countries such as India. In the 1990s India became one of the leading source countries for labor migration to the Middle East. These workers combined earnings from abroad with the income earned by family members at home to maximize their household income. Such models provide less insight, however, into the migrant decision-making among professional and highly skilled workers since opportunities abroad usually translate to moves of greater distance and the psychological, social and financial costs of leaving some family members at home often outweigh the benefits of moving the entire family abroad.

Micro-level economic models began to give way to more macro-level structural models that examine the social and economic structure within and between nations. Piore's (1979) Dual Labor Market theory represents one of the earliest models of this variety. According to Piore's theory "immigration is not caused by push factors in the sending countries (low wages or high unemployment), but by pull factors in receiving countries (a chronic and unavoidable need for foreign workers)" (Massey et al., op cit.). The basic contours of advanced industrialized countries, such as the United States, generate a dual labor market structure with high paying, high status positions at one end and menial, low paying jobs at the other end. This economic structure leads to immigration when natives either feel unwilling to take the low status jobs or lack the requisite skills to fill openings in higher skill-level occupations. In either case, employers must rely on more pliable sources of labor.

World Systems Theory (Wallerstein, 1974) offers one alternative to the Dual Labor Market Theory, which more directly relates to the conditions facing professional workers. This theory suggests that the predominance of capitalist modes of production in more developed countries encouraged the development of core and peripheral areas, which control the flow of goods and services and the production of raw materials, respectively. The penetration of capitalist systems into the peripheral, less developed, countries causes dislocations which lead their citizens to migrate either internally (e.g., away from an agricultural lifestyle and into cities to look for alternative forms of support) or internationally.

Although applications of the World Systems perspective often focus on the dislocations caused among agricultural classes, one analysis by Sassen (1988) provided important insights into how the process may operate among higher socioeconomic classes. According to Sassen, as the developed countries of the core moved into a post-industrial economic phase their economies became increasingly service oriented. The failure of these developed countries to train sufficient numbers of workers for service-related jobs created a demand for skilled labor from outside the "First World" societies. This model helps account for the demands for foreign-trained physicians in the late 1960s and early 1970s and for immigrant nurses in the 1980s and 1990s. It also offers some insight into the most recent influx of computer engineers in the late 1990s and the special legislative measures passed to facilitate (or, in the case of physicians, eventually to hinder) immigration among these professions.

As an outgrowth to the world systems perspective, Massey (1990) offers some ideas on how a process of demand for immigrant labor can become a self-generating cycle known as "cumulative causation." Massey's model offers the first significant insight into the role that immigrant social networks play in the immigration process. According to Massey, the dislocations caused by the penetration of capitalist modes of production into agriculture and traditional forms of income generation lead a migrant pioneer to immigrate abroad. That individual provides information and social and economic support to friends, family and fellow natives in his sending community, which eventually leads to further movements abroad. The cycle becomes self-perpetuating at some point such that the social networks of individuals become migrant networks providing the information and opportunities necessary to maintain a system of movement between core and peripheral areas.

A further outgrowth of the World Systems perspective and the migrant network concept appears in Fawcett's (1989) notion of

"Migration Systems." This framework takes Massey's model a step further and suggests that as migration flows become self-sustaining they develop stable components such that distinct migration streams develop between particular sending and receiving areas. These streams develop very intense flows politically (e.g., through bilateral trade agreements), socially (e.g., through the development of parallel educational institutions in the core and peripheral countries) and economically (e.g., through the exchange of specific goods and services). The Migration Systems Theory suggests, for example, a possible mechanism whereby the Philippines became one of the major source countries for medical personnel to the United States (Ong, Cheng and Evans 1992).

Prominent Conceptualizations of Social Networks
As already noted, Massey made important contributions to the application of social networks to the immigration process. A much earlier formulation, however, appeared in Mitchell's (1969) study of networks as part of the migration process from rural to urban areas in African countries. Mitchell emphasized the relative position of an individual in a social network and the link between the individual's location and their access to information channels. According to this conceptualization, networks create and reinforce norms for social behavior. Mitchell's study, however, focused primarily on the structure of networks and their operation with respect to internal migration. Massey's work provided the first meaningful application of these concepts to the study of migration as an international phenomenon.

Massey's work generated a variety of attempts to expand on or modify the network concept. Bashi (1997) examined the migrant networks of West Indians and found that rather than operating as a direct-line, with information passed from one network member to another in an orderly fashion, a few select individuals became centralized in the migrant network. These key individuals acted as specialized sources of information and social support, forming "hubs" of migration-related services. According to Bashi, the migrant networks in these cases developed linkages through individuals ("spokes") relying on two or more hubs for migration support.

Findlay and Garrick (1990) presented a re-conceptualization of the network idea, which they called the "Migration Channels Framework." In their formulation, networks operate through intermediaries who channel information about opportunities abroad. These channels may develop through personal ties to family, friends and fellow co-workers or impersonal ties such as the media and advertisements in professional journals. The channels perspective bears close resemblance to a network framework but it eliminates the longitudinal aspects of the process[6]. A channel may exist independently of a particular individual (e.g., advertisements in professional journals) and may cease to play a role in the immigration process after the actual move.

More recently, Davern (1997) provided a generalized conception of social networks and urged application to a wider variety of social phenomena. In Davern's framework, networks operate through their structure, the resources available to the individuals involved, the norms which develop within the system and the longitudinal nature of social relationships. Applying these concepts to the study of migration allows for more diversified models of network operation. Davern's model offers the insight that the structures that encourage immigration lead to an infinite variety of migrant networks and not a single type of network dependent on a particular type of tie.

Gaps in Theoretical Knowledge
As discussed previously, the lack of coverage of immigrant professionals in the study of migrant networks leaves important gaps in knowledge of what conditions influence their immigration decisions, how professionals respond to structural barriers, what form their networks take and the constancy of those networks over time. Boyd (1989) specifically asked "To what extent do personal networks, represented not just by family but also by friendship and community of origin ties, play a role in corporate sponsorship in which immigration requires arranged and government approved employment?" (p. 649). In the same article, Boyd suggested a need for further study into methods

---

[6] The "channels" these authors describe offer information on opportunities abroad. The structure of recruitment for particular occupations (e.g., the lottery system used to assign physicians to hospitals for residency) may lead to the predominance of particular channels of occupational information among members of that profession. However, the channels framework does not address questions of whether or not those intermediaries remain part of the immigrant's adaptive network and whether these channels dictate the use of networks more generally.

of identifying the personal networks of individuals sponsored through occupational criteria and the extent to which the ties of occupational migrants encourage further immigration. The research which follows makes some attempt to address these issues as well as to answer the questions presented in the introductory section of this chapter.

METHOD
Theoretical
I attempt in this study to provide both a conceptualization of networks as well as an analysis of network operation. I assume that migrant networks exist not simply as links between family, friends and community members but as more complex structures. These structures "may not be connected to the migration process [itself] but become important structural support(s) when international opportunities become available to the [members of a particular] group" (Lindquist 1993: 81).

Analytical
Ideally, this study would utilize a more comprehensive methodological tool identified by Louis (1982) as incorporating survey research and ethnographic data collection. Massey (1987) and others used the "ethnosurvey," as it is called, to study migrant networks in their larger research projects but due to the time, cost and locational constraints it does not offer a feasible framework for the purposes of this study. Instead, I attempt to utilize a modified version of an ethnosurvey design. The study fails to collect data from the prominent sending regions and offers only a minimal longitudinal perspective but it does attempt to mix analysis of existing national data sets with data obtained through interviews with immigrant professionals.

Methodological developments in recent years encourage greater use of both qualitative and quantitative methods in the study of demographic phenomena (see, for example, the symposium on "Qualitative Methods in Population Studies" in the December 1997, issue of *Population and Development Review*). Knodel (1997) suggests the following benefits of combining qualitative and quantitative methods: 1) the capacity for qualitative data to "confirm or contradict survey results" (p. 850); 2) the ability of the researcher to "gain a fuller understanding of the meaning of survey findings" (p. 851) and 3) the contribution qualitative methods can make towards "finding an explanation for some of the relationships being studied" (ibid.). This study makes some attempt toward meeting these objectives through the use of statistical analysis of quantitative data sources, focus group research and personal interviews.

The first two analytic chapters utilize data from the Immigration and Naturalization Service and the United States Census Bureau. In these chapters I examine the impact of legislation on network usage and the impact of resources on immigrant settlement decisions. These data sets, however, suffer from various shortcomings, discussed later, which prompted some attempt to collect data through interpersonal questionnaires. Fawcett and Arnold (1987b) identified a number of problems in using personal surveys to study immigration including the inability to obtain an adequate sample and bias against those who chose not to immigrate and those who chose to return to their country of origin. However, interpersonal surveys provide the only tool for addressing some of the complex issues involved in network development and usage.

The research design leads to coverage of a wide range of data sources and aspects of the immigration process. In addition, by abandoning a pure case study approach, this research provides greater possibilities for generalization of network processes among professionals than would a study focusing on a particular ethnic group and particular occupation. The primary drawbacks to the design include the fact that it fails to provide the insights available from a true ethnosurvey and that it suffers from some lack of comparability when an attempt is made to match respondent characteristics from a variety of data sources. The analysis, although broader in scope than many past studies, also focuses on a limited number of occupations and, eventually, on only two prominent sending regions. The survey also provides only suggestive information given the very small sample employed.

CHAPTER SUMMARY

Chapter 2 presents the conceptualization of migrant networks utilized throughout the remainder of the study. The chapter begins with a discussion of the limitations of past models of migrant networks and moves on to discussion of the relevant elements of networks. The discussion draws heavily on Davern's (op cit.) formulation as outlined above. It applies Davern's concepts to the case of immigration and presents both a general framework for understanding migrant networks as well as two specific examples of how the framework applies.

The third chapter utilizes data from the Immigration and Naturalization Services' Public Use Files (1972-1992) in order to study the impact of legislative decisions and economic conditions on the migration patterns and network usage of migrants from a large number of sending regions. This analysis focuses heavily on longitudinal trends and offers systematic evidence that network usage differs depending on a large number of individual characteristics including age, sex and occupation. Findlay and Li (1998) documented differences in the channels used by migrants across occupational groups but did not attempt to study the impact of these channels over time. The analysis presented in this chapter, therefore, provides important insights into the development and use of migrant networks longitudinally.

In the fourth chapter I combine data from the INS with that from the 1980 and 1990 Census Public Use Microdata files to examine the settlement decisions of immigrants entering through alternative network ties. I consider the influence of several key resources, including the existence of established co-ethnic communities and favorable economic conditions, on those decisions. While the second chapter stresses the structural and longitudinal dimensions of migrant networks, this chapter attempts to address the role of resources in influencing the immigration process. The results suggest that resources in the destination country play an important role in sustaining migration flows to particular areas.

The fifth chapter combines information obtained through a focus group with data from a small-scale survey of Indian and Filipino professionals employed in one of the four occupations chosen for analysis in the New York City metropolitan area. In this chapter I intend to examine how professionals conceptualize the immigration process and determine what role networks play in individual decision-making. The focus group interview served to inform the survey and to determine the type of language professionals use to discuss their immigration experiences and their use of personal networks. Although the data collected through the focus group and the survey offer no more than suggestive evidence of the role networks play, they prove essential to the larger purpose of the study. Without supplementing the quantitative data with interpersonal surveys we would have no tangible evidence that networks actually exist among professionals (i.e., the existing national surveys offer no direct data on network usage).

The final chapter reviews the major findings of the study and suggests possible areas for further inquiry. My research indicates that a variety of networks exist among immigrant professionals and that the content and structure of those networks change over time. These changes come about in response to what Grieco (1998) termed the "migration auspices" ("the social, economic, political and historic contexts within which migration proceeds" p. 706) prevalent in the United States. The study suggests a need for further research into the operation of norms in the immigration process for professionals, the development of network contacts from the sending country and differentiation of migrant networks into a number of other adaptive types of network ties. The results of this project should encourage a future larger-scale survey of immigrant professionals.

CHAPTER 2
The Conceptualization of Migrant Networks

INTRODUCTION

The past twenty years saw a tremendous growth in the use of social network models to describe a variety of phenomena. Scott (1991) defined social network analysis as "a set of methods for the analysis of social structures, methods which are specifically geared towards an investigation of the *relational* aspects of these structures" (p. 39, italics in original). The network metaphor appears in studies of a broad diversity of subjects including job finding (Granovetter, 1974), corporate structure (Zeitlin, 1974) and immigrant decision-making (Massey et al., 1987). In many cases, however, researchers utilize the concepts from social network analysis without providing the requisite theoretical support to their arguments, i.e., they may describe a specific form of network, along with its particular elements, without identifying the underlying assumptions regarding that network's structure. Without some discussion of the more general network framework invoked to study a particular set of circumstances, the discussion remains limited to a specific research context. For example, a researcher studying the spread of gossip may identify a group of people involved, their inter-relationships and social positions, but if the analyst fails to specify the broader elements of the network, her model may not apply to studies of alternative forms of information exchange.

In part, the lack of generalizability may result from the relatively undeveloped state of the field of network analysis and the proliferation of terms and definitions arising in consequence. The set of methods associated with network analysis developed through three research traditions; sociometric analysis, the Harvard researchers of the 1930s and the Manchester school of anthropology (Scott, 1991: 7). Efforts to unite the methods, terms and assumptions into a broader field of study began only recently. However, despite some justifiable confusion in the use of network concepts, some scholars continue to accuse others of simply, "[invoking] 'the social network' as an incantation in praise of informal help supplied to individuals by kinfolk, friends and neighbors" (Wellman and Berkowitz, 1988). These charges hold true in many studies of immigration processes.

Theories of migration decision-making evolved from economic, individual-based models to those emphasizing broader societal units. As discussed in Chapter 1, the early push-pull theories (see, for example, Todaro, 1976) focused on choices made by individuals as part of a micro-economic strategy to improve living standards. From these models developed more macro-based models of global inequality (Piore, 1979) and the world system perspective (Wallerstein, 1974) which purportedly encourage immigration through the development of social and economic dependency between developed and developing countries. Although these theoretic alternatives viewed immigration as part of a macro-economic phenomenon, they retained an emphasis on individual-level decision making. In more recent work, researchers emphasize the household as the primary decision-making unit. For example, Massey (1988) and others explain immigration through the links that develop between individuals in the sending and receiving societies. In this formulation, network ties encourage immigration as a means of diversifying household economic functions rather than simply improving the living standards of those individuals who make the move abroad (Taylor, 1986, 1987; Massey 1990).

Massey's (1990) conceptualization views migration as a confluence of macroeconomic, structural and human capital theories with an emphasis on the joint effects of the sending and receiving socioeconomic contexts. As he describes it,

> "Macroeconomic and structural theories explain how social and economic institutions and distributions are transformed in different geographic regions to determine local opportunity structures, while human capital theory provides a way to explain how individuals make decisions within those structures" (ibid. p. 7).

In his model, social networks mediate the costs of migration and offer one strategy to increase household resources. The individual benefits through superior employment prospects and members of the household expect to benefit through the transmission of remittances from the immigrant worker to the home community. In other words, the networks which individuals share between source and destination areas operate through the structural environment to reduce the monetary and psychic costs of migration while increasing the information and opportunity benefits. According to Massey, "once the number of network connections in an origin area reaches a critical level, migration becomes self-perpetuating because migration itself creates the social structure to sustain it" (op cit. p. 8). Despite the rich insights Massey's model offers, his conceptualization of immigrant networking may not accurately reflect the experiences of all migrants; a point which I return to later.

Much of the research into migrant networks relies heavily on Massey's work to the detriment of a fuller understanding of network processes. One of the most serious drawbacks concerns the fact that a great deal of the work centers around the circumstances faced by Mexicans and immigrants from other Latin American source countries (Menjivar, 1997; Hagan, 1998), which biases conclusions against more distant sending regions. Although world travel does not consume as much time and expense as it once did, immigrants traveling from Asian countries, for example, incur greater costs than do those who enter the U.S. from a neighboring country. A second shortcoming in the application of migrant network theory results from the tremendous reliance on case studies, which focus on the experiences of less-skilled workers. Although some studies indirectly examined the experiences of skilled workers[7], few systematically studied the use of networks among immigrant professionals.

This chapter begins with the presentation of a general model of social networks. The first section outlines the basic elements of all networks and identifies several additional features useful for distinguishing network types. In the second section, I apply the model to the study of immigration and follow-up with a discussion of various forms of migrant networks. Using the concepts and models developed in this chapter, I intend to conduct an extensive analysis of network

---

[7] For example, some authors conducted comparative analyses of successive cohorts of immigrants from a particular sending country (Smith, 1976; Liu, Ong and Rosenstein, 1991). Due to the changing demographic and economic characteristics of members of these cohorts, these studies amount to a comparison of highly skilled and lower skilled immigrants.

usage among immigrant professionals and to determine how these networks aid professionals in immigrating and adapting to American society.

THEORY
What is a "Social Network"?
Social network analysis evolved in close correspondence with the field of structural analysis. From a structural perspective the network operates as the primary organizing feature of a society with the composition of network relationships influencing individual behavior. In the words of one structural analyst, proponents of this perspective examine

> "… the ordered arrangements of relations that are contingent upon exchange among members of social systems … [and] … map these structures, describe their patterns … and seek to uncover the effects of these patterns on the behavior of the individual members of these structures" (Wellman and Berkowitz, 1988: 3).

Under such a framework it becomes important to understand not only the basic elements of a particular social network but also the more general features which characterize the network's structure.

Despite the wide range of topics studied through the perspective of social network analysis all models incorporate the following two basic network properties: nodes and connections. These terms developed through the influence of sociometrics and graph theory on network analysis (for elaboration of these methodological approaches see Scott, 1991) but many applications replace them with the alternatives: actors and social ties, respectively. Utilizing these concepts, social networks represent, therefore, social systems in which actors (e.g., individuals, organizations or associations) interact through their relationships with other members of the system. The sociogram provides the most basic model of networks as individual points (representing the actors) joined by lines (denoting relationships). However, in most cases these diagrams oversimplify the form and content of social networks.

According to Davern (1997), aside from actors and ties, social networks incorporate four additional components. The first component, structure, signifies the actual content and shape of the network including the "strength of ties" between network members. In his seminal work on the topic, Granovetter (1973) defined "strength" as deriving from "a (probably linear) combination of the amount of time, the emotional intensity, the intimacy ... and the reciprocal services which characterize the tie" (p. 1361). Network structure characterizes the most essential additional property in that it defines exactly the organization of actors and their interrelationships. In a study of the exchange of gossip, network structure may include the individuals involved in the passing of information, as well as the target of the gossip, the relationships existing between members of the system and the degree of overlap in the relations between network members.

Resources represent the second component of networks. Members of every social system differ with respect to the amount and quality of resources they bring to a social exchange. The resource component identifies "the distribution within networks of various characteristics that differentiate among actors within society" and includes such characteristics as "ability, knowledge, ethnicity, estate, gender and class" (Davern, 1997: 289). Actors in similarly structured networks may possess differential resources such that those with greater resources obtain more favorable social or economic outcomes.

In the case of the gossip network, a victim of gossip with high socioeconomic status or privileged standing in a community may command the economic resources necessary to prevent rumors from reaching the level of public discourse. On the other hand, the same individual, owing to their social position, may face greater difficulty in preventing gossip from reaching the mass media than an individual relatively unknown in the community.

The normative component of networks arises in response to the underlying roles of agents within a social system. This third feature of networks includes the "norms and overt rules that influence the behavior of actors within varying networks" (ibid.). The development of norms depends crucially on the types of ties that exist between network members and directly relates, therefore, to network structure. The strength of ties signifies the quantitative durability of a tie but this strength depends on the qualitative nature of the relationship between actors. These two properties interact and reinforce each other to produce differing socioeconomic conditions. For example, reporters usually feel more compelled to pass on information regarding public figures than facts pertaining to "the Average American" as part of the normative structure of "newsworthiness."

The final component of networks identified in Davern's article, the dynamic component, "takes into account the opportunities and constraints for tie formation and the ever-evolving network structure" (ibid.). Unlike the previously discussed properties of networks, the dynamic component depends crucially on longitudinal data. Depending on the interplay of the remaining elements, the dynamic nature of networks manifests itself in terms of network stability. A particular network may thrive or collapse as network ties develop or break down, as norms influence member interaction or as resources affect the exchange of goods. Turning once more to the gossip example, as a scandal develops, interest may wane depending on the relevance of the information to community members such that fewer people remain a part of the network's active structure and those currently involved represent a selective sub-stratum of the population. Only by comparing the structure of the network over time would these changes be apparent.

Figure 2-1 pictorially illustrates the core components of networks as outlined from Davern's article. The boxes represent actors in the network with their connections depicted as either solid or dashed lines. These basic features define the general shape of the network with the thickness of the line signifying the strength of ties between actors. A solid line indicates a strong tie, such as would exist in a marital relationship characterized by a great deal of temporal, emotional and intimacy investment. A dashed line represents a weak tie (e.g., the relationship between two strangers seated next to each other on a flight). Lack of a line would indicate that no tie exists between those particular members of the network.

Directional arrows and the central purpose of the exchange represent the resource component of the network. Arrows on the lines indicate the relative power of one network member over another and the exchange of resources from one to another. The purpose of the social system, in conjunction with the direction of the exchange, informs the relative magnitude of resources. One may deduce the norms operating within a system through the interplay of actors and resources but they do not lend themselves to pictorial representation. Similarly, a single figure cannot capture network dynamism but comparison of a series of diagrams constructed over the course of time

Figure 2-1: Basic Network

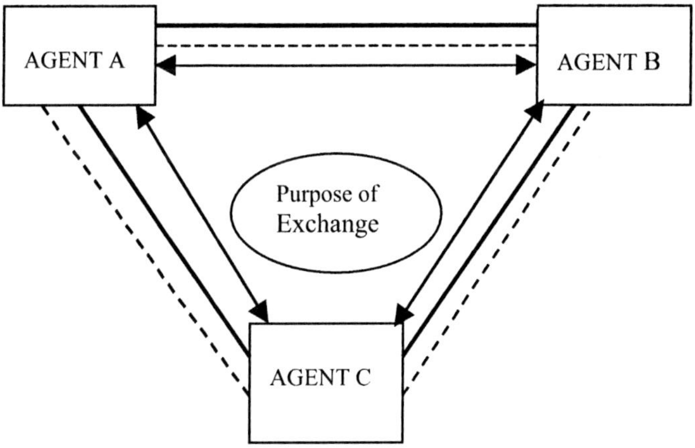

would indicate the changes that have occurred to the network, its members and its overall structure.

Social Networks and Immigration
As research into the content and function of networks gained in prominence, researchers began applying the methods and concepts to an increasing number of areas of inquiry including the study of immigration. However, a majority of the immigration-based studies evaluated only one or two of the aforementioned components of networks without regard to the importance or implications of the remaining factors. One of the earliest and most influential studies of social networks in the migration context was *Social Networks in Urban Situation: Analyses of Personal Relationships in Central African Towns* (1969) edited by J. Clyde Mitchell. In the introductory chapter, Mitchell defined a social network as "a specific set of linkages among a defined set of persons, with the additional property that the characteristics of these linkages as a whole may be used to interpret the social behavior of the persons involved" (p. 2). This definition focuses on the structure of networks but also recognizes the importance of that structure on influencing individual behavior.

Throughout the remainder of the chapter Mitchell's discussion reflects the sociometric perspective of networks popular at that time. He addresses two elemental forms of network qualities, morphological characteristics and interactional characteristics. Within these discussions he mentions the importance of obligations and the content of links, including the qualitative nature of ties. He also addresses the importance of the durability of ties, with the recognition that "rights and obligations are ... potential links ... which may come into being for a specific object and disappear again when that object is attained or frustrated" (op cit. p. 26); and the reciprocation of relationships. Mitchell, therefore, observed several of the same components of networks as identified in Davern's article but Mitchell's heavy reliance on graph theoretic concepts led to a rather inelegant model of migrant networks.

As mentioned previously, Massey significantly influenced the acceptance of social network concepts in immigration research through his contributions to migration theory. Massey (1990) defined migrant networks as "... sets of interpersonal ties that link migrants, former migrants and non-migrants in origin and destination areas by ties of kinship, friendship and shared community origin" (p.7). In his discussion of the "cumulative causation" of migration, which networks facilitate, Massey recognized the importance of the normative component of networks in his claim that "non-migrants draw upon [reciprocal] obligations to gain access to employment and assistance at the point of destination" (op cit. p. 8). The concept of cumulative causation inherently incorporates network dynamism as new ties come to complement or supplant the original set. However, Massey's research emphasizes strong ties between relatives, friends or community members. As discussed below, weak ties between would-be migrants in source countries and their sponsors in destination areas become important in a variety of contexts.

In another paper Waldorf (1996) suggests that migrant networks represent special cases of social networks with three primary functions. In addition to channeling information regarding the area of destination, migrant networks form the basis of social obligations and provide a foundation for future immigration through family reunification. Unlike either Mitchell's or Massey's work, Waldorf gives greater attention to the role that networks may play in return migration. Waldorf asserts that "every movement between origin and destination modifies the size and composition of the immigrant stock and thereby its aggregate power in influencing migration flows" (op cit. p. 648). Waldorf, therefore, recognizes the normative aspect of migrant networks but places greater emphasis on the dynamic character of these systems. In this formulation, network structure extends more fully between the sending and receiving areas with changes in the network structure occurring from both ends of the process and not simply in a linear fashion from the source to the destination country.

Finally, Fawcett and Arnold (1987a) discuss social networks as the basic micro-level linkage in their Migration Systems Paradigm. In their attempt to provide a more "comprehensive view of immigration processes" (p. 456), these authors suggest that a variety of linkages exist which influence individual immigration decisions. State-to-state (e.g., economic inter-reliance, laws and military aid) and mass culture (e.g., shared language and "Westernization") linkages shape the macro dimension of immigration. Family and social networks; including geographic dispersion of family or fellow natives in a destination country, the exchange of information and the existence of occupational niches operate at the micro-level to encourage or hinder individual migration.

Fawcett and Arnold offer an insightful conception of immigration processes and the role of networks within this system but fail to specify more precisely the character of these networks. Their list of the typical factors affecting networks, however, incorporates the four components emphasized in this chapter. Their discussion of geographic dispersion and the historical depth of migration provide evidence of network structure. The emphasis on communication, remittances and the socioeconomic status of previous migrants offers some insight into network resources. They specifically address the normative aspect of family obligations and their paradigm heavily emphasizes the dynamic nature of immigration processes.

Application of Davern's Concepts
In his paper, Davern (op cit.) presents some examples of ways in which to apply his concept of network configuration to the study of a variety of socioeconomic issues and encourages adaptation of these concepts to a wider body of analyses. In this section, I apply Davern's concepts to the study of immigration. Depending on individual circumstances, immigration usually involves the migrant and various federal agencies

including the Immigration and Naturalization Service. In the case of undocumented immigration, the act of immigrating may involve both the migrant and individuals in the host country who assist in adaptation. For individuals seeking entry through America's immigration preference system, on the other hand, one additional agent, the immigrant sponsor, becomes essential to developing a representative model of migrant networks.

The structure of migrant networks refers to the context of interrelations and, more importantly, the strength of ties between the participants. In the case of legal immigration, the ties that develop between migrants and individuals or institutions in the host country significantly determine their qualifications for visas. Since passage of the 1952 McCarran-Walter Act, American immigration law has emphasized two primary modes of entry, that which occurs through the sponsorship of employers and that which depends on relatives in the destination country. These two forms of sponsorship correspond, in most circumstances, to weak ties in the case of employment visas and strong ties for family-based visas[8]. The structural component, therefore, distinguishes between the two basic forms of entry as represented by American immigration law.

The resource component plays the greatest role in determining mode of entry. The level of individual resources among network actors affects not only who successfully locates a suitable sponsor in the destination country but also who qualifies to offer future sponsorship to potential immigrants. A variety of personal resources, including income, education and nativity[9], determine who obtains entry through one of the available legal channels. Professionals more often possess the financial and informational resources to enable them to obtain sponsorship through either strong or weak ties. Lower skilled workers, on the other hand, usually do not qualify for employment-based visas and, therefore, rely more heavily on familial sponsorship.

---

[8] Exceptions abound, particularly in the case of individuals who enter the United States and then begin working in a family-centered enterprise.

[9] Although country of birth does not play a very prominent role in immigration today, it proved a crucial resource under the quota laws of the 1920s. For example, the system of country quotas, fully abolished in 1965, set aside only a limited number of visas for Asian countries.

Some form of the normative component exists in every network regardless of the individual characteristics of system members. However, the strength and characteristics of norms likely differ depending on the types of ties involved. When migrant networks involve weak ties between migrants and potential employers, norms primarily dictate an exchange of sponsorship for service. Although the employer has a strong stake in the well-being of her employees, there is less normative pressure to look after everyday adaptive needs. On the other hand, normative expectations between an immigrant and his family dictate involvement at every level of the immigrant's life (e.g., social, economic, psychological, etc.). Norms similar to those for family-based immigrants likely hold for undocumented immigrants as well. In fact, the normative component may prove even more essential to individuals entering without legal documentation since they, and those who assist them, risk severe penalties for breaking the law.

The final element, the dynamic component, operates to influence network development. Over time new individuals must become involved in the migration stream otherwise the network breaks down entirely. The other dimensions of networks play important roles in determining in which direction the networks expand or contract. If the normative component encourages recent immigrants to naturalize and subsequently bring in additional family or friends then the network will likely expand throughout a particular sending area. On the other hand, if migrants make frequent temporary trips abroad without obtaining permanent residence then the network may stagnate. Finally, if the ties from migrants do not extend beyond their nuclear household then the network structure does not support a continuation of migrant sponsorship and the network may die out or simply take the form of something other than an immigrant network.

Specific Examples of Migrant Networks
Light et al. (1993) noted one problem with past analyses that utilize the network perspective. These authors claimed that, too often, scholars treat "one network as identical to another" (p. 39) despite the complex processes which underlie their development. The previous section sought to illustrate a general model of network structure. The present section utilizes this model to outline two possible applications to alternative migrant networks.

The first network, graphically displayed in Figure 2-2 and henceforth referred to as an "Employment Migrant Network," represents the type of network typical among those entering through sponsorship of a U.S. employer. In this example, the primary actors include the Immigration and Naturalization Service (INS), the Department of Labor (DOL), the foreign national and the potential employer. The INS and the DOL interact to determine who legally qualifies for employment visas. Employers must submit claims to these governmental bodies in order to bring in foreign-born workers. Depending on their reliance on immigration to fill labor needs, the interaction between employers and these institutions may occur once or many times. However, not all of the actors in the employment model directly interact through relational ties. For example, the Department of Labor plays an important role in awarding occupational visas[10], which need not directly involve the potential immigrant.

Weak ties predominate in this network with the exception of the link between the two governmental bodies who typically work together closely in assigning visas. In most cases, the individual immigrant in this network possesses a fairly high level of resources since a majority of the visas awarded through occupational preferences go to highly skilled workers. Within the network, however, the migrant holds a relatively weak resource base given their heavy reliance on the potential employer and fair application of the relevant legislation and procedures. Norms generally play a less significant role in this type of network except with regard to the expectations of employers, as discussed previously. The dynamic character of these networks may either manifest itself in change of employers or through further sponsorship of relatives under one of the family preference categories.

---

[10] The Secretary of Labor may add or remove occupations from the Department of Labor's Schedule A list of protected occupations, which may affect an individual's capacity to enter the United States but does not relate to that person's particular circumstances. More direct interaction does occur, however, in the sense that the Department of Labor oversees the certification process for all immigrants attempting to enter through an occupational preference category.

Figure 2-2: Employment Migrant Network

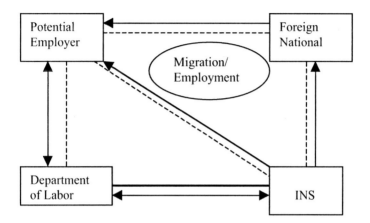

The aforementioned characteristics apply equally well to those individuals entering through immigrant visas and those entering through non-immigrant visas[11] with the exception of the dynamic component. Due to the temporary nature of non-immigrant visas the networks of individuals in these positions change frequently and in different ways than among immigrants. For example, non-immigrants often must return home before they are permitted to apply for permanent resident status. Depending on the period of time for the visa, the networks of non-immigrants likely change sooner than the networks of immigrants. On the other hand, non-immigrants do not have the option of changing employers while resident in the United States which could actually lead to more stable networks in the short term.

A second type of network frequently utilized by immigrants to the U.S. falls under the general heading of family-based networks and

---

[11] American immigration law distinguishes between those people admitted to the United States as permanent residents (i.e., immigrants) and those admitted for a temporary stay who must eventually return home or adjust to permanent resident status (i.e., non-immigrants). Non-immigrant visas include passes for business and tourism as well as temporary work permits.

refers to a "Spousal Migrant Network." This network involves a different set of actors than the employment migrant network. First, the Department of Labor has no role in the assignment of family-based visas. Second, sponsors for family visa must be directly related to the individual wishing to immigrate. Potential familial sponsors include spouses, parents, children and siblings. In the more specific form of family-based network discussed here, the migrant's spouse provides sponsorship. Figure 2-3 illustrates the basic properties of a spousal network.

Aside from the individual actors involved, another important structural difference between a spousal network and an employment network involves the types of ties. As noted above, marriage serves as the connection between actors in the spousal network. As one of the most elemental forms of strong tie, marriage suggests the potential for tremendous normative pressure to sponsor additional family members and to aid in adaptation to American society. Those immigrants seeking spousal sponsorship as single individuals enjoy relatively greater resources than do those entering through other family connections in that the former may, theoretically, choose from among the pool of all potential spouses assuming they have some opportunity to meet. The dynamic character of spousal networks often proves more important than employment-based migrations in that family-based migrants often attempt to bring in additional family members, perpetuating a type of chain migration.

Usefulness of the General Network Framework
The representation presented in the preceding sections should prove useful in a number of ways. First, as demonstrated in the examples provided, this delineation allows one to distinguish between several different types of migrant networks. Rather than limit the applicability of networks to one particular subset of migrants (e.g., unskilled, undocumented Mexicans), this model appears useful for describing every variety of network. Application to alternative migrant networks simply requires manipulation of the four key network components. Providing a more general framework allows for the development of network models that more accurately reflect reality. American immigration law identifies four primary categories of entries:

Figure 2-3: Spousal Migrant Network

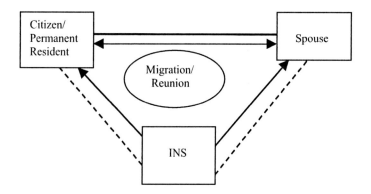

immigrants, non-immigrants, refugees and undocumented entries. The general framework presented here offers the flexibility to represent the networks of each of these groups. Additionally, this conceptualization allows for distinctions between the networks of a wide range of immigrant groups including unskilled and highly skilled immigrants, a fact essential to the remainder of this research. Finally, in general this model provides a more coherent view of the migration process from its initial stages to its culmination.

CONCLUSIONS

This chapter outlined a general model of social networks and applied these concepts to the study of immigration. It began with discussion of a 1997 article outlining the basic features of social networks and identified how to apply these concepts to the study of migration processes. Through examples of particular types of migrant networks, the chapter sought to demonstrate the greater usefulness of this conceptualization and the more accurate reflection of American immigration processes.

The analysis makes several contributions to the study of networks broadly and to the study of immigration more specifically. First, by examining the applicability of Davern's model to the study of immigration, this chapter expanded on potential uses for a new framework. Second, the models presented provide a more precise representation of migrant network formation and operation. For example, if a network fails to develop the "cumulative" characteristic Massey describes, evidence regarding the structure or other features of the network may indicate why it does not favor cumulative causation (e.g., the ties between actors do not extend beyond a nuclear household). Finally, this conceptualization provides the tools necessary to study a wider class of immigrants, including professionals, and to study more distant sending regions such as India and the Philippines; the primary areas of interest to the remainder of the study.

CHAPTER 3

Legislative and Demographic Impacts on Network Usage

INTRODUCTION

As discussed in the previous chapter, migrant networks provide an important conceptual tool for understanding the immigration process. Networks serve many functions and increase predictive power for determining who enters the United States and how they do so. However, the literature on migrant networks does not address an adequately representative cross-section of the immigrant population. Analyses within the field of immigration studies largely ignore the experiences of professional workers.

Interest in the reasons for and means of migrating among professionals peaked in the 1970s after passage of the 1965 Amendments to the Immigration and Nationality Act resulted in large numbers of Asian professionals immigrating to the United States. Fear of a "Brain Drain" undermining productivity in "Third World" nations led to a wide body of literature aimed at understanding its underlying causes and consequences. Although interest in professionals waned in the 1980s, it rekindled in recent years as United States policy makers contemplated changes in immigration legislation which would place more selective emphasis on immigrant skills.

In this chapter, I focus on two major modes of entry among professionals and examine how they operate across occupational classes. Specifically, I intend to address a number of issues. First, I will utilize the framework of migrant networks outlined in Chapter 2 to examine the immigration patterns of professionals. Next, I will show that past conceptualizations of migrant networks that emphasized close relations do not necessarily apply to professionals. In fact, even among professionals, differences in immigration patterns emerge across occupational groups. Finally, I discuss use of a broader view of migrant networks to capture the true complexity of immigration.

BACKGROUND
A Conceptualization of Migrant Networks

Social networks consist, most basically, of actors and the relationships that exist between them. To develop a feasible network framework, however, requires consideration of four additional properties, as outlined by Davern (1997) and discussed extensively in the previous chapter. To review, first, the structure of a network indicates its physical content including not only which ties exist but also the strength of those ties. The structure may include individual actors or corporations and describes the relationships between members of the system. The second property, resources, affects the relative power of network members and influences network operation. Resources help determine social and economic outcomes of the network and may include educational background, ethnicity, class or other individual characteristics. Norms dictate the reciprocal obligations between network members and play an important role in sustaining the network. Finally, every network operates through a dynamic component that defines the ways in which networks expand or contract over time as members enter and/or leave the system.

Utilizing this basic framework to study the immigration process and examining how these factors interact provides the means for describing a wide variety of migrant networks including those that facilitate undocumented entry and those based on family relationships. Past models of migrant networks emphasized strong ties to family and friends (see, for example Massey, 1990) but these conceptualizations do not necessarily apply to the circumstances faced by higher socioeconomic status migrants. Given their superior resources, higher socioeconomic status immigrants possess the ability to obtain information regarding potential visas in the destination country, to conduct extensive job searches and to visit the destination area before actually emigrating.

This chapter examines two particular forms of migrant networks, spousal migrant networks and employment migrant networks, and analyzes the effects of legislative decisions and economic conditions on their availability. Using longitudinal data from the Immigration and Naturalization Service, I describe the nature of migrant networks for a sub-set of immigrant professionals and show that even within this sub-set the use of networks differs considerably depending on individual characteristics. In this chapter I elaborate on some of the network components described above (e.g., to show how the properties of networks change over time) and demonstrate the importance of a flexible model of networks for understanding immigration as a process.

Legislation's Role in the Immigration Process

Immigration usually takes place through the aid of networks relying on either strong or weak ties. As described by Granovetter (1973) strong ties exist in relationships characterized by substantial time investment, high emotional intensity, intimacy and the reciprocal exchange of services. A marital relationship or that between a parent and child most clearly satisfies these requirements. Alternatively, low levels of time investment, weak emotional bonds, a lack of intimacy and an unreciprocated exchange of goods or services would characterize a weak tie. One might imagine the relationship between two strangers sharing a taxi as typical of a weak tie. Given these examples, purely strong and weak ties represent two ends of a continuum with some interactions falling more clearly towards one end than the other depending on the characteristics of the relationship.

American immigration policy developed in reflection of these general conditions. As the United States moved from an open borders policy to one of restriction, certain immigrant characteristics took precedence over others in awarding immigrant visas. In particular, immigrant skill level and relationship to an American citizen became the most important determinants of who obtained entry. Clearly, kin-based admissions reflect some form of a strong tie, as discussed previously. Immigration through skill-based visas most often occur through weak ties since, at least initially, among the qualities of strong ties mentioned earlier only a reciprocal exchange of goods (i.e., sponsorship for labor) necessarily exists between an employer and a potential immigrant employee. Legislative decisions, therefore, influence the availability of immigrant preference categories (Lobo and Salvo, 1998) and can, in turn, affect future use. In addition to the three major immigration acts passed since the 1920s, several smaller acts profoundly affected the distribution of visas to professional workers based on the two predominant types of ties.

The 1952 Immigration and Nationality Act (McCarran-Walter Act) made several important changes to immigration law as it held since the 1920s. Although the system of country quotas remained a part of the

1952 law, it was modified slightly to allow a token number of entries from Asian countries.

A more significant change was the introduction of a visa preference system. The new law favored family reunification by setting aside an unlimited number of visas for the spouses and unmarried minor children of citizens and assigning a large percentage of the remaining, restricted, visas on the basis of other family relationships. Among the numerically limited visas, the law set aside fifty per cent of a country's quota for those highly skilled workers whose services were in short supply among the native labor force and another twenty per cent for the spouses and unmarried adult children of permanent resident aliens. Legislators also introduced specific visas for other relatives of United States citizens (e.g., including parents and unmarried adult children) but assignment to these categories depended on under-subscription of the primary visas.

The McCarran-Walter Act, therefore, had significant implications for the availability of ties to immigrant sponsors. The preference system assured that two particular modes of entry gained prominence, each representing one of the two types of ties Granovetter described. Potential immigrants could either utilize their family connections (i.e., strong ties) to obtain a visa or find an employer willing to sponsor them under an occupational category (i.e., through a weak tie).

The 1965 amendments to the Immigration and Nationality Act entailed a complete overhaul of immigration law by replacing the country-based quota system with hemispheric ceilings. The law awarded 170,000 visas to individuals originating from Eastern Hemisphere countries (with a 20,000-visa limit per country) on the basis of a revised preference system and 120,000 to persons from the Western Hemisphere on a first-come-first-served basis[12].

Changes in the preference system from its 1952 version resulted in some hindrances to employment-based immigration. As shown in Table 1-1 (page 4), the new system broke down the occupational provision into two separate categories; assigning only twenty per cent

---

[12] In 1976, Congress further amended the Immigration and Nationality Act to bring the Western Hemisphere under the same system of preferences and apply the 20,000 per-country limit. In 1978 the separate ceilings for the Eastern and Western Hemispheres were combined into one worldwide limit of 290,000 but this number fell to 270,000 in 1980.

of all numerically restricted visas (i.e., 34,000 visas) on the basis of skill level. In addition, the priority level for occupation-based visas was reduced from first (under the unified category) to third and sixth (following the 1965 changes). In addition, the law stipulated that the Department of Labor must ensure no immigrant worker would either replace an American worker or adversely affect the wages or working conditions of similarly employed individuals in the United States[13].

The act continued to favor immediate relatives of U.S. citizens and permanent residents as immigrants but two basic changes to the preference system magnified this effect. First, parents of U.S. citizens could now enter outside the numerical restrictions. Whereas the 1952 law limited parental visas, along with visas awarded to unmarried adult children of citizens, to thirty per cent of each country's quota, the 1965 amendments reserved an unlimited number of visas for the parents of American citizens. The new law also brought several new family relationships into the visa preference system, including brothers/sisters and married children of U.S. citizens.

The 1965 amendments also introduced provisions for refugees and certain special immigrants such as ministers of religion. These provisions essentially added new types of migrant networks to the immigration system. However, the number of entries in these classes formed such a small percentage of total immigrants (e.g., only six percent of the numerically restricted visas went to refugees) that familial and occupational migrant networks retained their predominant position.

A third general piece of legislation, passed in 1986[14], diminished the attractiveness of marriage as a form of family-based network. The Immigration Marriage Fraud Amendments sought to discourage the

---

[13] The Eilberg Act, an amendment to the Immigration and Nationality Act, altered the Department of Labor requirements for occupational visas. The act introduced the requirement that third preference beneficiaries must obtain a job offer prior to immigrating and that potential employers, rather than the Department of Labor, secure proof of a labor shortage in their field before hiring an immigrant worker. Both of these provisions further increased the difficulty of obtaining sponsorship through an American employer.

[14] The Immigration Reform and Control Act also passed in 1986 but had relatively little impact on the migration of professionals so I omit discussion of it here.

misuse of spousal visas through dubiously contracted marriages - those entered into solely for the purpose of immigrant sponsorship. The amendments require a two-year waiting period before issuance of a spousal visa. During those years, the potential immigrant qualifies as a conditional permanent resident and at the end of the period, if the immigrant can provide evidence of an intact marriage or a sincere effort to maintain the marriage, they may petition to have the conditional status removed. Passage of the Marriage Fraud Amendments led to reduced reliance on one form of family tie as a means to immigrate and bolstered usage of other types of networks.

A more recent legislative measure, the Immigration Act of 1990, had the greatest impact on the availability and use of migrant networks by professional workers. More than any other act before it, the 1990 law clearly delineated the preference classes by the strength of social ties. Apart from the approximately 65,000 visas set aside for diversity immigrants[15] and asylees, legislators formally divided the preference classes into "Family-Sponsored" and "Employment-Based" categories. The 1990 law increased the worldwide ceilings on immigration to 700,000 between fiscal year 1992 and 1994 and reduced it again to 675,000 beginning in fiscal year 1995. Although the family-sponsored preference categories remained the same as those in the 1965 amendments, the overall increase in the immigrant ceiling dramatically increased the absolute number of individuals entering through family ties.

The most significant change in the 1990 law as it applies to professionals, however, resulted from the addition of three new occupational preference categories. The new employment-based visas provide immigrant opportunities to persons of exceptional ability, individuals willing to invest in businesses to provide employment opportunities and other "special immigrants." Whereas the 1965 law awarded no more than 34,000 of all immigrant visas on the basis of

---

[15] The diversity program awards visas to individuals from those countries "adversely affected by the 1965 Immigration and Nationality Act Amendments" (U.S. Immigration and Naturalization Service, 1997). A transition period from 1992 to 1994 reserved 40,000 visas for diversity immigrants - 40% of which were allocated to natives of Ireland. Once the program came into permanent effect, in fiscal year 1995, the total number of visas reserved increased to 55,000.

skill, under the new law employment-based entries account for over 146,000 of the preference visas. These changes led to a dramatic increase in the number and percentage of all immigrants entering through employer sponsorship.

Differential Usage of Migrant Networks by Occupation

The general impacts of the legislative measures outlined above do not hold for every category of professional worker. Differences in the demographic characteristics of individuals typically employed in a particular profession may lead to differences in the use of networks. For example, if differences exist between men and women in their use of network connections then legislative measures which alter the set of available visas could affect the nursing profession, or some other female dominated profession, differently than a profession, such as engineering, which is dominated by men.

Another obvious source of difference in network usage across professions has been the passage of legislation that specifically targets particular subgroups. For example, the Health Professions Educational Assistance Act of 1976 greatly curtailed immigration by foreign medical graduates (FMGs) through removal of most health professions from the Department of Labor's Schedule A list of certified occupations and the introduction of qualifying exams. With occupational channels effectively blocked for foreign-trained physicians, one would suspect that in the years following passage of the Health Professions Act use of family networks would increase more dramatically for physicians than for other professionals. Physicians faced an even more hostile immigration environment after passage of the 1986 Marriage Fraud Act. With employer-sponsorship unlikely and with greater scrutiny of immigrant-citizen marriages, most foreign-trained doctors were entirely dependent on other family members for admission.

Unlike physicians, foreign-trained nurses benefited from a labor shortage over the 1980s and 1990s. Several measures made it easier for nurses to qualify for employment visas or at least to gain entry through non-immigrant visa categories and later adjust to permanent resident status. Unlike workers in other medical specialties, professional nurses appeared on the Department of Labor's Schedule A from its inception onward, which made the labor certification process relatively easy. In addition, the Immigration Nursing Relief Act, which passed in 1989, allowed certain qualified nurses to adjust from non-immigrant to permanent resident status without regard to numerical limit and established a new non-immigrant category to encourage further migration of registered nurses.

Finally, two acts, passed in the fall of 1992, provided immigration benefits to two more groups of workers. The Chinese Student Protection Act allowed those nationals from the People's Republic of China staying in the United States between June 4, 1989 and April 11, 1990, to adjust to permanent resident status under a special class of employment-based preferences. A second act provided some of the same benefits to scientists from the independent states of the former Soviet Union and the Baltic States. Although not substantial in a numerical sense, the passage of these acts highlights the special treatment that occasionally befalls particular occupational classes.

Figure 3-1, based on data from the Immigration and Naturalization Service, shows the number of immigrant professionals admitted between 1959 and 1995[16], delineated by occupational group. The data presented clearly reflects the legislative environment. The graph indicates a relatively egalitarian system of admissions in the early 1960s. Engineers and nurses were admitted in only slightly larger numbers than doctors and scientists before passage of the 1965 Amendments. The trend lines indicate marked changes after 1965, however, with spikes in the number of admissions for engineers and nurses in 1968. Physician admission increased suddenly in 1970 and remained high until 1977, just after passage of the Health Professions Act. Nursing admissions show an increase after 1989, the year of the Nursing Relief Act. The most dramatic increases occur in 1992, the year the Immigration Act went into effect. With the exception of physicians, each of the occupational groups displays a sharp increase in admissions between 1992 and 1993. Finally, the figure graphically illustrates the overall increase in immigrant professional admissions over time.

---

[16] Data for fiscal years 1980 and 1981 are missing due to processing errors at the INS.

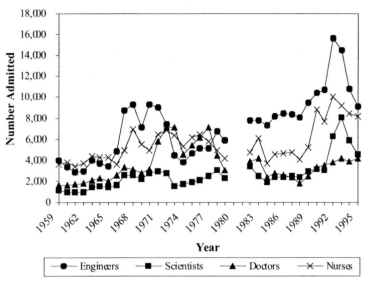

Figure 3-1: Professionals Admitted to the United States, Selected Occupations: 1959-1995

Source: Immigration and Naturalization Service (1959-1995)

The prior discussion and graph clearly outline how legislative measures can interact with demographic, political or economic conditions to alter the pattern of migration across sub-groups within a larger occupational class. Although the laws discourage physicians from immigrating to the United States through either of the migrant networks emphasized in this study, they encourage nurses to utilize employment networks. In the analytic section of this chapter I formally model these differences and test a number of hypotheses.

Because the legislative measures discussed previously place progressively greater emphasis on immigrant skills, longitudinal analyses should indicate increased significance of weak ties in more recent years. The first model, described later, tests this hypothesis for the entire sample.

Given the differential treatment of professionals in the legislation passed, we should find significant differences in the use of strong-versus weak-ties by occupation. Specifically, physicians should exhibit the greatest reliance on strong ties and nurses the most dependence on weak ties. Engineers and scientists most likely fall in between these two extremes but, given the demand for computer engineers in the U.S. labor market, engineers likely enter through weak ties to a greater extent than scientists. A second set of models test this hypothesis using the full data set as well as through occupation-specific longitudinal analyses.

Gender differences in the use of networks likely interact with other individual characteristics and political-economic circumstances to influence the types of ties predominating in an immigration stream. Although men generally utilize weak ties in their professional interactions to a greater extent than women do, a legislative environment favoring the immigration of nurses through occupational skills could alter these patterns. In general, I expect to find men more likely to enter through weak ties but in examining occupation-gender interactions I expect female nurses to utilize weak ties more extensively than their male counterparts.

As the "world economy" has become more interdependent, structural changes in the supply and demand for labor has created occupation-specific migration channels favoring certain sending areas over others. In addition, historical impediments for particular geographic areas and a variable marriage market can influence the availability of familial sponsors. A final set of models examines the relative likelihood of entering through strong- or weak-ties by sending region. I expect Western Europeans to enter through strong ties to a greater extent than others, followed by Eastern Europeans, Latin Americans, Africans, Middle Easterners and Asians; with the latter most dependent on weak ties.

DATA AND METHODS
Data Set Strengths and Weaknesses
This study utilizes the Public Use Files, *Immigrants Admitted to the United States,* of the Immigration and Naturalization Service (INS) for

fiscal years 1972-1996[17] to examine use of networks among professionals. Most studies of networks utilize qualitative data collected through personal surveys in order to capture the complexity of the migration process. Reliance on quantitative data does not permit an analysis of networks in the traditional sense but does offer insights into specific aspects of network usage; in this case structure as it pertains to the admissions process. Combining this set of findings with analyses of alternative aspects of the immigration process should facilitate a more complete depiction of professionals' network utilization.

Aside from the fact that use of the INS files limits analytic capabilities, these data suffer some additional weaknesses. First, there is a problem concerning the report of occupation. In some years a large number of individuals fail to provide their occupation and, among those who do, the meaning of this designation depends on the class of entry. For those entering on an employment visa, occupation refers to the job they will perform in the United States. On the other hand, among non-immigrants adjusting status, the variable indicates the individual's current occupation. For every other type of entry, occupation refers to the last job held in the immigrant's prior country of permanent residence (Tomasi and Keely 1975)[18]. Another serious problem with the occupational designation concerns the coding of this variable across years. For the first ten years, the INS coded occupation according to the detailed occupation codes utilized by the United States' Census Bureau. In the following years, the INS consolidated these categories into twenty-five descriptive codes. Without information from the INS as to the procedure used to map the detailed codes into the 25 categories[19] no means exist to assure that the data for a particular occupation refers to the same population for the entire study period.

---

[17] Lack of access to the full set of data files in the time available led me to limit the analysis to these years.

[18] A related problem concerns the fact that the definition of occupation may differ between the sending and receiving countries such that the report of occupation as "engineer" may mean different things for individuals entering in each of these immigrant status groups.

[19] I know of some attempts by other researchers to obtain this information from the INS but, to my knowledge, the system of coding remains unspecified.

Finally, the INS data include missing cases on a number of variables for several years. For example, the FY 1979 file contains missing information for 10 variables on 22,680 records, including information on sex of the respondent - a possibly important predictor of network usage across occupations. Unfortunately, the only way to handle the problem entails dropping those cases for which the relevant data do not exist.

The Public Use files may suffer some serious drawbacks but, for the purposes of this analysis, offer information superior to other data sources. Most importantly, the data set covers the population of interest; immigrants admitted to the United States. The usual alternative sources, the United States Census of the Population and the Current Population Survey (CPS), do not distinguish among the various classes of immigrants. In these sources undocumented immigrants, legal immigrants and non-immigrants all fall into the generic category of "foreign born." In addition, the Census and CPS do not record the class of entry, which would render it impossible to examine the use of networks among recent immigrants. Finally, the INS files cover annual admissions over the fiscal year calendar[20], which enables more detailed analyses of longitudinal trends.

Dependent and Independent Variables
The following analysis attempts to discern the impact of several major legislative decisions on the use of spousal versus occupational migrant networks among a subset of professional workers. This research examines the hypothesis that network usage differs according to a variety of individual characteristics including occupation, sex, immigrant status and region of birth. I chose four professions for the study based on the large percentages of immigrants entering in each of the occupational categories over the period in question. According to

---

[20] In 1977 the INS altered the calendar period for the fiscal year from July 1 through June 30 to October 1 through September 30. As a result, although each INS Public Use file contains twelve months worth of data, they do not cover the same months before 1976 and after 1977. In addition, July 1, 1976 through September 30, 1976 did not fall into either FY 1976 or FY 1977 so the INS designated the period as a Transitional Quarter. For the purposes of this analysis I assigned the 1976 Transitional Quarter data to either FY 1976 or FY 1977 using a random number generator.

data compiled from the 1990 United States Census, the following professions contain the highest percentage of foreign-born workers: engineering, the natural sciences and mathematics, nursing and medical sciences (Bouvier and Simcox, 1994).

Based on the discussion of migrant networks presented in the previous chapter I limited the analysis to those immigrants who entered the United States through one of the two primary network ties (i.e., spousal or occupational). For individuals without family members in the United States, spousal- and employment-based sponsorship represent the only two possible means of entering the U.S. By excluding other types of family-based entry, therefore, the study examines more comparable admission categories. Limiting the analysis in this way also eliminates the need for calculating the probability that an individual immigrant possesses family connections in the destination area, the inclusion of which would require a different set of models and assumptions.

Finally, I also limit the analysis to new arrivals. The INS data provide information regarding those individuals who adjusted status from a non-immigrant (i.e., temporary) visa to an immigrant (e.g., permanent resident) visa but there are two potential problems in utilizing the data on status-adjusters. First, those non-immigrants included in the data set are selective of all non-immigrants. Only those who successfully adjust status gain admission and are included in the INS files. Second, from previous analyses (see Bagchi, 2001) it is clear that status-adjusters and new arrivals utilize very different networks. For those adjusting status we only know which was their last non-immigrant visa. We do not know how many or which other visas these individuals held previously and, more importantly, it is impossible to determine the structure of their networks when they first entered the U.S. Including both immigrants and non-immigrants would, therefore, confound the results.

Since direct data on network usage do not exist in most quantitative data files, the class of admission variable recorded in the INS files can serve as a proxy for network type. Re-classifying this variable into the desired categories enables modeling the odds of choosing one type of visa over another. I grouped individuals entering as primary beneficiaries[21] of occupational visas into a single category of "Employment-Based Admissions" and those immigrants entering as spouses of U.S. citizens in "Spousal Admissions." The dependent variable, therefore, contrasts these two modes of entry; taking on the value one if the immigrant arrived on an employment visa and zero if they entered through a spousal visa.

The independent variables fall under two general headings: legislation and individual characteristics. The legislative measures include most of those discussed in the previous section of the chapter. Since the data set begins in the year 1972 the analyses exclude the 1952 Immigration and Nationality Act and 1965 Amendments. For the remaining laws a dichotomous indicator identifies those years before and after the law went into effect[22].

The Marriage Fraud Act, the Nursing Relief Act and the Immigration Act of 1990 should all exhibit a positive relationship with the odds of entering under an employment visa. As marital visas became more difficult to obtain, potential migrants most likely turned to other visa categories. This would lead to an increase in the number seeking entry through occupational skills. Both the Nursing Relief Act and the Immigration Act introduced new categories of admission and eased entry through employment-based categories, therefore, after their passage we should see some increase in entrance through these visas.

Passage of the Health Professions Act and the INA amendments would most likely lead to reductions in employment certification since both limit the number of admissions for previously unrestricted classes of entry (i.e., physicians and immigrants from the Western Hemisphere). In addition, although combining the hemispheric ceiling led to an increase in the percentage of all visas awarded on the basis of

---

[21] For most visa classes, entries fall into one of two categories: primary beneficiaries refer to those aliens "on whose behalf the visa or petition is directly filed" while derivative beneficiaries include the "spouse(s) or child(ren) of the principal beneficiary" (Papademetriou and Yale-Loehr, 1996: 39). The analysis includes only primary beneficiaries.

[22] I used the effective date of the law rather than the year of the law's passage since, in some cases, the effective date falls several years after the passage date.

occupational skills[23], it could not sufficiently offset the increase in number of entries among spousal visas. Therefore, both laws should exhibit a negative relationship to the odds of entry under employment categories.

The personal characteristics variables were all constructed using dummy variables. The analyses consider only those individuals reporting their occupation as a physician, nurse, engineer (including all sub-fields but excluding engineering technicians) and scientist (broadly defined to include all natural scientists, computer scientists and mathematicians). The occupation code, therefore, contrasts each occupational category with the remaining three. Immigrant sex assigns the value one to males and zero to females. Area of origin was operationalized using country of birth. As alluded to earlier, the dummy variables contrast six regions (Western Europe, Eastern Europe, Latin America, Asia, Africa and the Middle East) with Eastern Europe representing the comparison group. Finally, the analysis also includes only those immigrants between the ages of 21 and 65. Very few immigrants entered under one of these occupational titles outside this age span and since these years represent the prime working ages, 21 and 65 appeared the most reasonable cutoffs.

Model Estimation

The analyses examine two of the four components of networks as identified in previous sections of the chapter: structure and change over time. Comparison of two types of networks, spousal and occupational, based on strong and weak ties, respectively provide some limited evidence of network structure. Using data for FY 1972 through FY 1996 indicates how these structures change over time. Without more detailed personal information on recent immigrants (unavailable in the INS files) we have no way of examining the role of resources or norms in network formation.

---

[23] The old system awarded a worldwide total of 290,000 visas and limited employment visas to 20% of the visas for the Eastern Hemisphere (i.e., 20% of 170,000 or 34,000 visas). However, this represents only 8.53% of the worldwide total. After combining the hemispheric ceilings and placing the Western Hemisphere under the same set of visa restrictions, the new law set aside as many as 58,000 visas on the basis of employment (20% of the full 290,000 visas).

I ran a series of logistic models, based on the following general equation, to examine longitudinal trends in the odds of entering the United States through an employment visa versus a spousal visa and to assess the impact of legislation and personal characteristics on those odds:

$$\log(\text{Employment Entry/Spousal Entry}) = Y_i = a_i + B_iX_i + e_i$$

(where X_i represents a matrix containing the set of independent variables included in the analysis). The first two models examine yearly trends in visa usage for all newly arrived immigrants. One model presents the findings on a yearly basis while the second adds controls for the legislative measures. A second set of equations examines the role of occupation and sex (and explores likely interactions) on the odds of employment visa utilization. The last two models consider the influence of origin area and also look for interactions with sex.

Results and Test of Hypotheses

Table 3-1 provides descriptive statistics for the relevant independent variables. Comparing the percentage of immigrants utilizing spousal versus employment visas indicates that while a large number of immigrants enter through both types of visas, professionals rely somewhat more heavily on their occupational skills to come to the United States. This suggests that previous conceptualizations of migrant networks, which emphasize strong ties, do not necessarily apply in the case of those immigrant professionals lacking previous U.S.-based family ties. The networks these individuals utilize appear much more complex than previous scholars implicitly suggest.

The table also shows a near even split in the data by sex. Looking at the figures for occupation we see that nurses and engineers predominate, accounting for the gender equity. Finally, while Latin Americans and Western Europeans make up a fairly sizeable portion of the immigrants admitted, Asians by far outnumber all other origin areas, accounting for over half of the entire sample.

Table 3-1: Descriptive Statistics for Independent Variables

Variable		Number	Percentage
Visa	Spousal	48,625	43.76%
	Occupational	62,487	56.24%
Sex	Males	60,312	54.28%
	Females	50,800	45.72%
Occupation	Doctors	19,913	17.92%
	Nurses	39,972	35.97%
	Engineers	38,472	34.62%
	Scientists	12,755	11.48%
Region	Eastern Europe	3,795	3.42%
	Western Europe[a]	25,408	22.87%
	Asia	56,138	50.52%
	Middle East	6,868	6.18%
	Africa	5,305	4.77%
	Latin America	13,598	12.24%
Mean Age		33 Years	NA
Total		**111,112**	**100%**

a - Includes Australia and Canada

Source: Immigration and Naturalization Service

Table 3-2 reports the results of the model describing annual trends in the odds of visa usage across the study period both with and without controls for the legislative measures. The bold faced, italicize dates reflect years in which one of the major pieces of legislation went into effect. I anticipated declines in the odds of employment-base entry for 1978 and 1979, the years that the Health Professions Act and the 20,000-visa country limit of the Immigration and Nationality Act (Health Professions and INA) and the Immigration and Nationality Act amendments to combine the hemispheric ceilings (INA and World Ceiling) took effect, respectively. Although the odds ratios reflect some decline it appears as a continuation of a trend begun earlier. Possibly, the environment turned negative towards immigration before passage of the laws such that a trend toward decreasing reliance on employment sponsorship started before the law took effect, although we cannot verify or refute this hypothesis with the available data.

A much clearer outcome exists with respect to the increase in the odds of employment entry relative to spousal entry in 1987, the year the

Table 3-2: Annual Trends in the Odds of Employment Entry
With and Without Legislative Effects, FY 1972 – 1996

Year	Odds Ratio	
1972	2.97**	3.41**
1973	2.63**	2.63**
1974	2.85	2.85**
1975	3.47**	3.47
1976	2.86	2.86**
1977	1.70**	---
1978	1.13**	2.27**
1979	1.12**	2.06**
1980	1.00**	1.84**
1981	0.86**	1.58**
1982	1.17**	2.14**
1983	0.99**	1.81**
1984	1.09**	2.00**
1985	0.92**	1.69**
1986	0.98**	1.80**
1987	1.18**	3.39
1988	1.18**	---
1989	1.16**	3.34
1990	1.05**	---
1991	1.14**	3.71*
1992	1.63**	16.00**
1993	1.20**	11.81**
1994	0.94**	9.20**
1995	0.35**	---
1996	0.25**	2.45**
Health Professions and INA	---	1.70**
INA and World Ceiling	---	3.74
RN Relief	---	3.02**
Marriage Fraud	---	2.17**
Immigration Act	----	1.13**
-2 Log Likelihood	**144,263.58**	**144,192.34**

* - Significant at the 0.05 level ** - Significant at the 0.01 level

Source: Immigration and Naturalization Service

Marriage Fraud Act took effect. After many years of decline in the odds of employment-based entry, use of employment visas returned to the level of the early 1970s. The results support the hypothesis that by limiting the availability of spousal sponsorship immigrants began to rely more upon potential employers or other types of visas. Passage of the Nursing Relief Act (RN Relief) in 1989 did not alter the trend very much despite a further increase in 1991.

By far the most dramatic result is the tremendous increase in the odds of employment entry in 1992 (the year the 1990 Immigration Act took effect). The model that includes the legislative measures indicates that in 1992 professionals in the chosen occupations were 16 times more likely to enter through employment visas than spousal visas. Since citizen spouses have always been permitted to enter outside numerical restrictions, passage of the 1990 Act did not affect this category of admission. However, as discussed in an earlier section, the law significantly increased the number and percentage of visas available based on occupational skills. With these facts in mind the magnitude of the increase is perhaps not surprising. However, the effect appears somewhat temporary, with the odds declining steadily back to more "normal" levels by 1996. Overall, the findings lend convincing support to the hypothesis of shifting trends in network usage over time and the growing significance of occupational skills.

Unlike previous analyses of migrant networks, this study examines the structure of networks not only within a broad occupational class (i.e., professional workers), but also between members of various professions. Assuming that factors which influence occupational distribution also lead to differences in the use of networks, one set of analyses tests for differences across professions. The findings, reported in Tables 3-3 and 3-4, confirm that the networks among various professional workers vary and that they do so in the expected manner. The odds ratios reported in Table 3-3 suggest that, when compared to the patterns observed for scientists, physicians rely more heavily on spousal sponsorship while nurses and engineers utilize employer sponsorship to a greater extent.

Table 3-3: Odds of Employment Entry by Occupation

Variable	Odds Ratio
Doctors	0.80**
Nurses	1.77**
Engineers	1.25**
Scientists	1.11**
-2 Log Likelihood	150,125.64

** - Significant at the 0.01 level   *Source: Immigration and Naturalization Service*

The occupation-specific longitudinal analysis presented in Table 3-4 provides a more detailed image of network trends. Across all four occupations, use of employer-sponsorship is high throughout the early 1970s (although this holds less true for scientists). Passage of the Health Professions Act profoundly affected both physicians and nurses but clearly impacted doctors more heavily. From 1977 until the Marriage Fraud Act took effect in 1987, physicians were actually more likely to obtain entry through spouses than through employers. Nurses were similarly affected in the years immediately following the Health Professions Act but this effect dissipated over the early 1980s. With decreased competition for employment visas from the medical professions, engineers and scientists saw immediate gains in occupation-based entry. However, passage of the Immigration Act in 1990, as seen from the earlier analysis, clearly had the most influence on network usage among these professionals. Nurses and engineers, in particular, found an environment in the early 1990s which overwhelmingly favored employment entry. As these two tables show, legislative measure significantly altered the set of available network ties and did so in an unbalanced manner across occupational groups.

Table 3-4: Annual Trends in the Odds of Employment Entry by Occupation, FY 1972 – 1996

Year	DOC	NUR	ENG	SCI
1972	2.35**	3.53**	5.00**	2.14**
1973	2.27	2.14**	4.08*	1.56*
1974	2.99*	4.35*	2.32**	1.00**
1975	3.87**	5.43**	2.70**	1.05**
1976	2.93*	4.97**	1.89**	0.86**
1977	---	5.97**	3.61**	1.61*
1978	0.60**	---	---	---
1979	1.06**	0.96**	7.25**	4.71**
1980	0.95**	0.50**	7.74**	5.48**
1981	0.59**	0.62**	6.77*	4.86**
1982	0.54**	1.49**	7.58**	5.27**
1983	0.57**	1.06**	7.12**	4.53**
1984	0.41**	1.33**	6.08	7.18**
1985	0.43**	1.06**	5.43	5.43**
1986	0.35**	1.35**	5.20	5.85**
1987	3.59**	2.63**	5.65	2.09
1988	---	2.81**	5.62	2.11
1989	1.81	---	---	---
1990	---	---	3.71**	1.90
1991	2.90	3.30	---	---
1992	---	32.34**	40.65**	8.77**
1993	2.07	22.39**	29.46**	9.00**
1994	1.72**	22.05**	16.13**	5.77**
1995	0.95**	8.17**	---	---
1996	1.01**	---	4.19	2.87
Health Professions/INA	2.21	1.78**	1.07**	0.84**
INA and World Ceiling	2.59	6.30**	4.62	1.09**
RN Relief	1.65*	3.47	5.58	1.86
Marriage Fraud	0.31**	2.35**	5.09	6.61**
Immigration Act	4.87**	0.45**	0.95**	0.81**
-2 Log Likelihood	**23,255.7**	**48,445.8**	**49,599.5**	**17,288.8**

* - Significant at the 0.05 level ** - Significant at the 0.01 level

Source: Immigration and Naturalization Service

An analysis of potential gender differences in network usage suggests that immigrant sex does not dictate network patterns. As shown in Table 3-5 above, men and women are equally likely to enter the U.S. through employers. However, further models test for possible interactions between sex and other individual characteristics.

Table 3-5: Odds of Employment Entry by Sex

Variable	Odds Ratio
Women	1.30
Men	1.27
-2 Log Likelihood	**152,297.70**

Source: Immigration and Naturalization Service

Table 3-6 examines interactions between sex and occupation. Taking female scientists as the excluded group, the data indicate that males in the four professions utilize weak ties to a far greater extent than do women, with the exception of nursing. Nurses, regardless of sex, enjoy a very favorable environment for occupation-based sponsorship. The odds ratios suggest that female doctors face the greatest obstacles to skill-based immigration, which could translate into unfavorable employment outcomes after arrival.

A test of the significance of these models indicates that adding interactions between sex and occupation to the individual equations improves the fit of these models considerably. The difference in -2 log likelihood values between the occupation model and the model including sex and the relevant interactions terms equals 2,172 while the difference between the model for sex and that including interactions amounts to 3,954. With degrees of freedom of four and six respectively, the more complex model significantly improves the fit over the more basic equations. Based on the findings in Tables 3-3 through 3-6, it appears that a variety of individual factors influence the structure of professionals' networks besides the legal environment potential immigrants face.

Table 3-6: Odds of Employment Entry by Sex and Occupation

Variable	Odds Ratio
Female Doctors	0.38**
Female Nurses	1.76**
Female Engineers	0.52**
Female Scientists	0.81**
Male Doctors	1.07**
Male Nurses	1.65**
Male Engineers	1.35**
Male Scientists	1.26**
-2 Log Likelihood	148,343.37

** - Significant at the 0.01 level *Source: Immigration and Naturalization Service*

The final set of models tests for the influence of sending region on network usage. Using Eastern Europe as the excluded category, the data reported in Table 3-7 indicate that Asians and individuals from the

Table 3-7: Odds of Employment Entry by Region of Birth

Variable	Odds Ratio
Western Europe	0.54**
Eastern Europe	0.46**
Latin America	0.43**
Asia	3.02**
Africa	0.89**
Middle East	1.10**
-2 Log Likelihood	134,157.39

** - Significant at the 0.01 level *Source: Immigration and Naturalization Service*

Middle East are the exceptions with respect to employer-sponsorship. Whereas most of the professionals in this study rely on citizen spouses to sponsor their entry, Middle Easterners and (especially) Asians dominate in the awarding of employment visas. However, I suspect that these odds mask important gender differences across regions.

A final model, which tests for gender-region interactions, confirms prior expectations. As seen in Table 3-8, when East European females serve as the reference group every other group meets with greater success in locating an appropriate employer-sponsor. Comparison of patterns for men and women within regions indicates that only Latin

Table 3-8: Odds of Employment Entry by Region of Birth and Sex

Variable	Odds Ratio
Western European Women	0.32**
Eastern European Women	0.16**
Latin American Women	0.71**
Asian Women	3.03**
African Women	0.71**
Middle Eastern Women	0.58**
Western European Men	0.75**
Eastern European Men	0.90**
Latin American Men	0.27**
Asian Men	3.00**
African Men	1.02**
Middle Eastern Men	1.28**
-2 Log Likelihood	**131,828.13**

** - Significant at the 0.01 level   *Source: Immigration and Naturalization Service*

American men obtain spousal sponsorship more frequently than their female counterparts and that men from the remaining regions experience much greater success in capitalizing on their occupational skills to gain admission to the U.S.

DISCUSSION AND CONCLUSIONS
Theoretically, this chapter sought to clarify the concept of migrant networks. As noted in the introductory sections, past studies of migrant ties constrained themselves to particular countries of origin, socioeconomic classes and specific modes of entry. Use of the case study offers important insights into the process of immigration and its complexity but limits the generalizability of findings. Researchers either must expand the number and variety of case studies performed or utilize other research methods in order to develop a more representative conceptualization of immigration and its underlying structure. To these ends, I extend the present research in the remaining chapters to

incorporate additional quantitative analysis and sample survey methods. Ultimately, I seek to study these processes through a simplified version of the ethnosurvey approach; one that examines the problem using a variety of techniques from several fields including sociology, survey research and demography.

The current analysis addresses two primary questions. First, do differences in the structure of networks exist among immigrant professionals? Second, does the structure of these networks change over time? The results from logistic regression models suggest an affirmative answer to both question. Operationalizing employment migrant networks and spousal migrant networks using entries through occupational preferences and visas for citizens' spouses, the analysis offers evidence that different types of networks exist across professions and that a variety of conditions affect the structure of these networks over time.

The regression results suggest the need to conceptualize immigrant networking as a process highly dependent on the circumstances of particular groups and circumstantial conditions. In an attempt to draw generalized conclusions, researchers often oversimplify the process they hope to explain. The evidence most clearly supports a need for further study into differences in network usage across occupations, between the sexes and by sending region.

Gender appears to play a very significant role in the process of immigrant network development. Although this chapter addressed only one stage of the immigration process (i.e., admittance to the host society), gender differences emerged with respect to both occupational and regional patterns. In examining both sets of factors the results confirm that males obtain employer sponsorship to a greater extent than similarly situated females. This could have important implications for later stages of the immigration process. For example, if immigrant women professionals must rely on family members for admittance they may face poorer prospects for locating employment after their arrival. Entry through an employment visa ensures that the sponsored immigrant receives the opportunity to capitalize on their occupational skills since it requires a job offer before arrival.

This discrepancy in the odds of entry between men and women may reflect the predominant view of women as dependents of men in the migration process (Morokvasic, 1984). The fact that most people continue to view men as the primary breadwinners, and due to the sometimes highly disproportionate sex distribution in the occupations under consideration, the results should not seem surprising. However, as discussed above, these patterns could have disastrous effects on female immigrants as they attempt to adapt to their new environment. Rather than alienating women further (e.g., the results suggest that the legislation passed to restrict physician immigration had much harsher effects for women) the U.S. government should design policies which mediate negative outcomes for those immigrants who come to the U.S. to settle.

In addition to the preceding, this research suggests several additional questions worth consideration and study. First, do employment (i.e., weak tie) entries eventually become strong tie migrant networks? The law currently awards employment visas to two different types of immigrants: the principal beneficiary and derivative beneficiaries. Among principal beneficiaries, those persons immigrating through employment sponsorship may sponsor relatives in large numbers within or outside the preference system thereby creating a family-based migration stream from a previously weak tie network.

Weak tie networks could sustain themselves over time but might take on different structural elements. For example, if a company hires an Indian engineer and particularly likes the skills and training of its employee the managers may decide to hire another individual trained in the same institution, leading to some type of informal recruitment system. A strong tie may develop through the employer and the particular institution from which they recruit but the ties between employers and employees remain essentially weak in nature.

A second, more fundamental question, pertains to the issue of how networks differ between those initiated by an employment visa and those by some type of family visa. Even if the process of migration changes in the ways suggested above, it becomes important to identify both the short run and long term differences in network operation. Weak tie migrant networks may attract higher socioeconomic status persons than strong tie migrant networks or vice versa. Assortative mating, for example, may ensure similarity in socioeconomic status between spouses but this correlation may dissipate as a migration chain develops. One of the greatest debates with respect to immigration policy concerns the question of whether or not immigrant skills have declined over time. Understanding the operation of both weak and strong tie networks may aid in predicting and understanding these outcomes.

The conceptual model of network development set forth in the first and second chapters provides much scope for further study of these and many other issues. The analysis pertains to a very specific set of immigrants but offers intriguing clues as to the various ways that migrant networks develop and operate over time. In addition to limiting the analysis to particular occupational groups, the study also focused on a small sub-set of modes of entry. Further research could cover a much broader range of topics, immigrant groups, visa types and individual circumstances. The analytic results clearly confirm the need for a flexible model of network development, one that adequately accounts for the broad patterns that result from so complex a process.

CHAPTER 4

The Network Ties of Indian and Filipino Immigrant Professionals

INTRODUCTION

Among the countries losing professional workers to the United States, India and the Philippines represent two of the most important due to the large numbers of immigrants involved. Especially in those professions with the highest percentage of foreign-born workers (i.e., nursing, medicine, engineering and the sciences), Indians and Filipinos arrive in the largest numbers. These countries also, therefore, serve as the most promising candidates for a detailed analysis of the role networks play in the immigration process among professionals.

Analyses of professionals' visas in the previous chapter provided evidence that migrant networks differ considerably across a range of individual characteristics, most significantly sex and occupation. The earlier chapter examined individual-specific factors, as well as the legislative environment in the United States. The present chapter utilizes data for only two nations and examines the roles that a variety of resources play in professional migration.

The analysis draws upon Fawcett and Arnold's (1987) Migration System Paradigm. In addition to their model of the immigration process, these authors discuss a number of factors assumed to affect that process at various stages. This chapter attempts to operationalize several of those resource-based measures in an attempt to assess their impact on networking among immigrant professionals. The general research questions guiding this chapter follow: 1) Do personal relationships or economic conditions play a more predominant role in locational decision-making among recent immigrants?; 2) What differences exist in these effects across occupational groups, by nativity and over time?; and 3) What do the findings suggest about the significance of migrant networks among highly skilled immigrants?

BACKGROUND
Immigration of Professionals from Asia
Immigration of professional workers to the United States did not begin
in large measure until the 1930s and 1940s when, due to political
turmoil in Europe, many Nobel Prize winning scientists and scholars
moved to the U.S. (Fortney, 1972). However, the numbers entering
remained relatively small until passage of the 1965 amendments to the
Immigration and Nationality Act. The emphasis on immigrant skills
and the elimination of national quotas affected skilled worker
immigration in two ways. First, it led to a dramatic increase in the
numbers of professionals entering the United States, with the
percentage of all immigrants reporting a professional occupation up to
11.5% in 1967 as compared to 3.1% in the period from 1926-1930
(ibid.). Figure 4-1, based on data from the Immigration and
Naturalization Service, demonstrates this growth between 1959 and
1995 (see footnote number 16 on page 42). Despite some precipitous
drops between 1970 and 1990, the general trend shows a steady
increase.
  The 1965 act also led to a substantial growth in the number of
Asians entering the United States, with a concomitant growth in the
percentage of Asians in the immigrant professional population.
Including all professional, technical and kindred workers, data from the
Immigration and Naturalization Service indicate that Europeans fell
from 37.1% of the immigrant labor force in these occupations in 1964
to 22.3% in 1970. Similar declines occurred among North and South
Americans while immigrants from Oceania remained at around 1.0% of
all such workers. Over the same period of time, however, immigrants
from Africa grew from 1.4% of the total to 6.7%, while Asian
representation exploded from 9.7% in 1964 to 52.9% in 1970 (Westoff
and Parke, 1972).
  Despite the fact that entry through occupational preferences
declined after the early 1970s in favor of family preferences (Arnold et
al., 1987), Asians continued to predominate the inflows of immigrant
professionals in the 1980s and 1990s with around 50% of all
professionals entering from Asian countries (Kanjanapan, 1995).
Within the broader class of immigrant professionals, certain
occupations particularly stand out for the high percentages of Asian

**Figure 4-1: Immigrant Professional, Technical and
Kindred Workers Admitted to the U.S., 1959-1995**

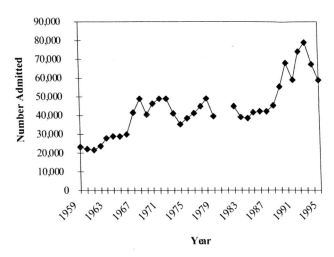

Year

Source: Immigration and Naturalization Service

immigrants within their ranks. These occupations comprise the four
under consideration here: engineers, scientists, physicians and nurses.

Due to a variety of unique influences, in every year since passage
of the 1965 act India and the Philippines represent two of the top five
contributors to the immigrant professional population (Liu, 1992).
Specifically within the occupations under consideration, Indians lead
all other Asian groups among immigrant engineers and natural
scientists, while Filipinos predominate in the medical field, particularly
within the nursing profession. Overall, Indians figure predominantly in
all four professions, while only among the natural sciences do Filipinos
fail to reach the top five in Asian sending regions. Historical
circumstances and political relations between the United States and
India and between the U.S. and the Philippines account in large
measure for the substantial contribution of these countries to the United
States' professional worker pool.

Indian Professionals Immigrate to the United States

Despite the lack of strong political and economic ties between India and the United States over the last two decades, Indian professionals have consistently made important contributions to the American workforce. Although Indian immigration to the United States started as early as the 1800s, it did not reach significant numbers until the early 1900s. The large scale immigration of Indian professionals, often referred to as the "Brain Drain," began in the 1950s but did not become a point of concern until the 1970s, after passage of the 1965 Immigration Act amendments accelerated the trend toward professional immigration (Melendy, 1977). A variety of factors appear to account for the increase. One of the most significant entailed passage of a law in 1962 restricting immigration into the United Kingdom from its former colonies. Given the close political ties between India and Britain, the U.K. had served as a primary point of destination for Indians wishing to emigrate. Once the U.K. discouraged this migrant route, Indians had to look elsewhere for opportunities. With the United States easing restrictions at about the same time, much of the immigration flow diverted to the U.S.

Additional legislative measures encouraged immigration of Indians from particular occupations in the 1960s and early 1970s. Until the passage of the Health Professions Act in 1977, the shortage of medical professionals in the United States led to heavy reliance of the American economy on foreign-trained physicians and nurses. Prior to 1977, both doctors and nurses appeared as special classes of workers on the Department of Labor's Schedule A list of protected occupations. In addition, the U.S. had suspended qualifying tests to screen Indian medical graduates for internships and residencies (Domrese, 1970). The passage of the Health Professions Act in 1977 eliminated these provisions and substantially curtailed the immigration of not just Indian physicians but all physicians, as discussed in Chapter 3.

The aforementioned political and legal factors, in part, account for the substantial contribution of Indians to the American professional workforce, but conditions in India itself suggest reasons why professionals sought opportunities abroad. Several authors suggest that the immigration of professionals from India does not meet the definition of a "Brain Drain" simply because the Indian economy produces more professionals than the labor force can absorb (Clark, 1970; Minocha, 1987; Ishi, 1987). Rather than depriving India of its highly trained workforce, these authors suggest, the U.S. simply provides an outlet from unemployment or underemployment. Minocha (op cit.) reported on several studies which showed that many Indian scientists could not find employment within their occupations and that those physicians and engineers who could find jobs usually started in low status positions with reduced pay and less responsibility.

In addition to the lack of opportunities at home, cultural patterns, established during the period of British rule, encouraged emigration from India, while historical patterns led to the predominance of professionals in the late 1960s migration flows. Throughout Asia, the United States and Britain established secondary educational systems which emulated Western standards, encouraged the use of English as a medium of learning and emphasized standardization of mathematics and science on a worldwide scale (Liu, 1992; Cheng and Yang, 1998). In many ways, the skills obtained in institutions following Western traditions translated into more lucrative careers in Western settings than in the Indian economy. Liu (ibid.) suggested that the lack of a sizable Indian community in the United States prior to passage of the 1965 amendments meant that Indians initially relied heavily on the occupational preferences to gain entry. Subsequent assortative mating created a propensity for Indians to attract other high socioeconomic status migrants.

Filipino Professionals Immigrate to the United States

Similar factors account for the immigration of Filipino professionals to the United States, although political ties between the United States and the Philippines played a more important role than in the case of India. Like India, the Philippine educational system developed along Western educational patterns (Ishi, 1987; Ong, Chen and Evans, 1992). The system encouraged English language fluency and required math and science programs to meet Western standards. However, several additional factors played very significant roles in the migration of professionals from the Philippines to the United States. As a former colony, Filipinos entered the U.S. freely as nationals until 1935 (Melendy, 1977; Gardner, Robey and Smith, 1985; Madigan and

Pagtolun-an, 1990). The political and economic ties between the two countries, as well as a system of cultural influences set up by the American colonizers, maintained the pattern of immigration long after the Philippines attained its independence and after American immigration law removed the restrictions on Asian immigration[24].

According to Ong, Chen and Evans (1992), the Philippines represents a prime example of Buroway's (1972) migrant labor system. According to this theory, a system develops between a core society and its dependent peripheral nations whereby the reproduction of labor becomes separated geographically from its primary area of use. The prime example cited in the case of the Philippines concerns the training of nurses and doctors to meet labor demands in Western nations. Without adequate demand for medical professionals in the Philippines, individuals trained in these occupations represent a system of labor developed for Western consumption. A second set of authors support this contention, suggesting that the Philippine government purposefully trains an excess number of individuals in "Western appropriate techniques" (especially in the medical profession) in order to encourage emigration and the remittance of wages to boost the Philippines' failing economy (Madigan and Pagtolun-an, 1990).

Other authors suggest that American influence on the Philippines' culture encouraged the acceptance of American values and social systems. According to Melendy (1977), the Pensionado Act of 1903 established an educational program that sent young Filipinos to the United States to learn American culture and social systems in order that they might return to the Philippines and spread American values. Espiritu (1996) suggested that a "Colonial Mentality" remains in effect in the Philippines, which encourages Filipinos to view American culture as superior to their own. According to Espiritu this "mentality," along with poor political and economic conditions in the Philippines, accounts for the large-scale immigration of Filipinos to the United States.

---

[24] As discussed in Chapter 3, passage of the 1965 Amendments to the Immigration and Nationality Act led to elimination of the "Asia-Pacific Triangle" and other country-specific quotas which had heavily curtailed Asian immigration.

As in India, a lack of opportunities for satisfactory employment at home and more lucrative job prospects abroad account for much of the movement from the Philippines (Ishi, 1987). As early as the 1960s, professionals and other skilled workers, such as engineers, pharmacists and physicians, accepted jobs as office workers and lab assistants due to high levels of unemployment in their fields of training. More recently, the Philippine economy took a serious downturn in 1984 after the assassination of Senator Benigno Aquino. From that time forward, the supply of skilled professional labor outpaced the economy's absorptive capacity (Carino, 1996). The presence of Filipinos in the U.S. prior to passage of the 1965 amendments may have encouraged some family migration, but these economic circumstances meant that many Filipinos sought entry through the available occupational preferences as well (Liu, 1992).

The nursing profession presents a special case of the situation in the Philippines, particularly given the fact that the Philippines operates as the major source of foreign-trained nurses in the U.S. According to Ong and Azores (1994), the severe and chronic shortage of nurses in the U.S. (due both to a growth in the demand for health care services and economic fluctuations in the United States) in part accounts for the migration of Filipino nurses to the U.S. This demand benefits from an oversupply of nurses in the Philippines. Despite historical and widespread out-migration of Filipino nurses, a lack of demand and poor economic conditions left over from the Marcos regime encourages a continual surplus. In addition, few restrictions on emigration exist within the Philippines while at the same time special preferences and legislative measures favoring those with foreign-training encourage nurses to immigrate.

Significance of Resources to Network Ties
As conditions in the United States, India and the Philippines led to systems favoring immigration of professionals into the United States, network ties became important in facilitating movement. As pointed out earlier, the networks of Indians developed primarily through weak ties to employers willing to sponsor skilled workers under the two occupational preferences of the 1965 Immigration Act amendments. On the other hand, Filipinos made use of both family connections and

employment prospects in the U.S. Over time, while employment migrant networks retained their significance to Indians and Filipinos wishing to enter the United States, family-based migrant networks have come to predominate net flows.

The last chapter examined networks through immigrant sponsorship with the assumption that individuals entering under spousal visas rely primarily on structurally strong ties and that those utilizing occupational preferences depend mostly on weak ties. This chapter examines conditions in the receiving society as an influence on network usage. Hence, while the last chapter emphasized the structure of immigrant professionals' networks, this one examines the resources available to migrants in the destination country. In this chapter, resources include access to fellow-natives, favorable employment conditions and familiarity with the environmental conditions in the area of destination. Given the availability of a suitable migrant network, the resources mentioned above help determine how successful an immigrant becomes in the immigration process and, eventually, in adapting to the new environment.

The present chapter examines the locational decisions of recent Indian and Filipino immigrants entering through spousal and employer sponsorship in an attempt to determine how resources affect their immigration. Historical patterns of immigration and settlement led to disproportionate growth in Asian communities within particular states. Table 4-1 (reconstructed from Table 4.2 in Barringer et al., 1993) shows the top ten states of residence for Indians and Filipinos in 1980 and 1990. The data depict two important trends. First, Filipinos settled in far more clustered a manner than Indians, with nearly half of all Filipinos resident in California in both years. Second, the figures suggest a more mobile population among Indians with much less stability in the rankings for individual states than among Filipinos.

In general, one would assume that most immigrants choose to settle in areas where previous immigrant natives reside, where job prospects appear favorable and where the environmental conditions match as closely as possible those of their home community. However, in addition to potential differences in the impact of these factors by nativity, important differences may exist by occupation within nativity

Table 4-1: Top Ten States of Residence:
Indians and Filipinos, 1980 and 1990

	Rank	1980 State	%	1990 State	%
Indians	1	New York	17.5	California	19.6
	2	California	15.4	New York	17.3
	3	Illinois	9.7	New Jersey	9.7
	4	New Jersey	7.9	Illinois	7.9
	5	Texas	6.0	Texas	6.8
	6	Pennsylvania	4.4	Florida	3.9
	7	Michigan	4.0	Pennsylvania	3.5
	8	Maryland	3.6	Maryland	3.5
	9	Ohio	3.5	Michigan	2.9
	10	Florida	2.9	Ohio	2.6
Total Pop.		*387,223*		*815,447*	
Filipinos	1	California	45.8	California	52.0
	2	Hawaii	16.9	Hawaii	12.0
	3	Illinois	5.7	Illinois	4.6
	4	New York	4.6	New York	4.4
	5	Washington	3.3	New Jersey	3.8
	6	New Jersey	3.1	Washington	3.1
	7	Virginia	3.0	Virginia	2.5
	8	Texas	2.0	Texas	2.4
	9	Florida	1.9	Florida	2.3
	10	Michigan	1.8	Maryland	1.4
Total Pop.		*781,894*		*1,406,770*	

Source: Barringer et al. (1993) Table 4.2 "

groups. For example, if an occupational niche develops within a specific nationality group recent immigrants may settle in an area with large numbers of co-ethnics with less concern for general employment conditions.

As another example, if labor shortages exist among the native labor force in a particular occupation then immigrants trained in that occupation may choose to pursue improved employment opportunities rather than focus on settling near fellow-natives. The circumstances members of the medical professions face likely lead to such an outcome. Especially in the case of foreign-trained physicians, market demands dictate where a physician may practice. Physicians trained in the United States benefit through placement in preferred settings. Foreign-trained physicians often must fill labor shortages where demand exists but where native-trained physicians do not wish to go.

We should also expect to see some differences by sex and by admission class. Chapter 3 demonstrated that occupation and sex can interact such that men generally obtain employer-sponsorship to a greater extent than women. Those entering through spousal sponsorship likely emphasize the presence of co-ethnic communities. On the other hand, since obtaining an occupational visa requires a job offer, those entering through employer sponsorship should respond more to the employment conditions in a particular state. Taken together, these points suggest that employment opportunities should have a greater impact on male professionals (with the exception of nurses), while the existence and size of native populations should affect women more.

Finally, changes brought about by legislative decisions suggest that economic conditions have gained in significance over time as compared to general environmental conditions. Immediately following passage of the 1965 amendments, Asian immigrants relied heavily on aid provided by fellow-natives already resident in the United States, who often lived in insulated communities and in only a handful of states. Under these conditions, new immigrants depended on the exchange of information offered by their fellow-natives. Over time, as the Asian communities in the U.S. grew and expanded into a larger number of areas, information channels and knowledge of opportunities increased such that knowing people in a certain area no longer proved as essential in successfully adapting to American society. Given this pattern of events, economic opportunities should prove more important than native communities in time periods further removed from the relaxation of immigrant restrictions.

Although family-based entry increased after 1965, native-communities likely play a less important role for two reasons. First, the literature review in the previous chapter discussed important legislative changes in the 70s, 80s and 90s that have eased entry for foreign-born professionals. These measures provided numerous means of entry for professionals outside the family preferences. Second, the following analysis considers only those professionals entering through either spousal or employer sponsorship. Limiting the analysis in this way effectively discounts the impact of increases in other types of family-based entry (e.g., sibling sponsorship).

A similar analysis, conducted by Vasegh-Daneshvary et al. (1986) and based on the 1980 Census Public-Use Microdata files, focused on college-educated immigrants (those with at least two years of college training) who entered the U.S. between 1970 and 1974 and who participated in the U.S. labor force in 1980. These authors found significant differences in the factors influencing initial choice of residence across origin regions. Among Asians, the variables relating to employment opportunities (i.e., state unemployment rates, research and development expenditure and number of scientists) proved more significant than for other origin regions. However, the presence of co-ethnics proved significant across all sending regions.

The Vasegh-Daneshvary et al. study, however, confounds the impact of these variables across very diverse immigrant populations. Treating Asia as an origin area undermines our ability to distinguish settlement patterns by very distinct sociocultural groups. A state such as California may support a very large Asian population but if Indians represent a small percentage of this group then it is misleading to say that California's foreign-born Asian population influenced the settlement patterns of recent Indian immigrants. Similarly, if state-specific unemployment rates differ significantly by occupation, then the overall state unemployment rate could represent a flawed indicator of the employment conditions for specific occupational groups. The analysis which follows addresses these and other potential problems in the previous study and offers some evidence of the changing significance of these factors over time.

Based on the above assumptions, the analyses in this chapter examine four hypotheses with respect to the settlement choices of recent Indian and Filipino immigrants in the United States. First, because professionals typically make a greater time and financial investment in their occupational training than other classes of workers, we can expect them to place high priority on utilizing their skills. With this in mind, professionals should generally be drawn to areas where unemployment rates are low and income potential is high. This suggests that, for the entire sample, employment opportunities should play a more important role than environmental factors in determining patterns of settlement for professionals.

With the legislative environment generally improving for occupation-based entry, employment conditions should become a more relevant factor in determining settlement decisions in more recent time periods. Although the number and types of familial admission categories expanded and currently face high demand (particularly among Indians and Filipinos), spousal visas have become more difficult to obtain under the current legal system. These facts give further credence to the idea that more recent immigrants give greater weight to employment prospects than the marriage market in deciding where they will live.

As noted earlier, Indian immigration is a more recent phenomenon than Filipino migration. With potentially fewer relatives in the U.S. from whom to draw on for aid, we should expect to find a stronger relationship between employment conditions and state of residence among Indians than among Filipinos.

Finally, employment-related factors should prove more predictive of settlement decisions among those groups making greatest use of employment visas. As such, female nurses and male engineers and scientists should demonstrate greatest dependence on economic factors. In Chapter 3, physicians stood out for their reliance on spousal sponsorship, particularly female doctors. In the case of physicians, therefore, the presence of co-ethnics should prove the most important determinant of residential decisions.

DATA AND METHODS
Data Set Strengths and Weaknesses
The present analysis utilizes data from both the 1982 and 1992 INS files, *Immigrants Admitted to the United States,* and the 1980 and 1990 *Public Use Microdata Samples* (PUMS) of the United States' Census Bureau. The INS files provide data on immigrants admitted to the United States, while the census files offer evidence of social and economic conditions within the fifty states and the District of Columbia. Both sets of files provide the respondents' place of birth as

a means of identifying Indian and Filipino respondents for the sample. Operationalizing ethnicity in this way may lead to errors since persons of non-Indian or non-Filipino ancestry (e.g., Europeans born in India) may appear in the birth place records. However, these cases do not occur in large numbers. Although the census data provide some means to weed out these aberrant cases, the INS files do not. Therefore, for the sake of compatibility, place of birth served as the indicator of ethnic background for both data sets.

I discussed the general strengths and weaknesses of these two data sources in Chapter 3. However, for the present purposes, several points bear further mention. The analyses in this section seek to explain immigrant residential decision-making as a function of conditions in the receiving society. Since the INS data cover annual immigrant admissions but the census occurs in 10-year intervals, the analysis focused on only a few years. In this case, I matched data from the 1980 and 1990 census files with data for 1982 and 1992 immigrant admissions. Two facts suggest the need for the time gap between the sets of data used. First, ideally the Census Bureau collects data for those U.S. residents present in a particular location on the day of the census administration, April 1[25] of the calendar year. The INS, on the other hand, utilizes a fiscal year beginning October 1 of a given year and ending on September 30 of the following year. Given the overlap between calendar and fiscal years, a two-year separation between data collection provided the minimal necessary time delay[26]. Second, immigrants considering moving to the United States likely examine the conditions in the U.S. before immigrating. Since most immigrants experience a time lag between the time they decide to migrate and the time they actually obtain a visa, the state-specific factors included in the analysis had to be measured prior to the immigrant's entry.

---

[25] In practice, the census actually covers people throughout the census year due to the necessity of follow-ups from non-return of the mailed census forms, refusals, empty residences and a variety of additional problems.

[26] Data for fiscal year 1981 would include some immigrants actually admitted in the fall and winter of calendar year 1980, so 1982 represents the first year of data for immigrant admissions independent of the data from the census files.

As noted earlier, proper analysis requires data from the census files for each state and the District of Columbia. The 1980 and 1990 PUMS files lend themselves to this type of extraction due to their organization by state codes. The Census Bureau, however, organized the 1970 file according to a three-fold hierarchy of specificity (i.e., geographical area, household and individual). The household level files omit personal information, so it is impossible to calculate, by state of residence, ethnic-group specific values of the independent variables. For this reason, I limited the analysis to 1980 and 1990.

A further problem with the INS files is that the variable "Place of Intended Residence" does not necessarily indicate the actual place of residence upon entry to the United States. Although somewhat problematic since an immigrant may choose to move immediately upon admission, given the limitation of the analysis to only spousal and occupation-based admissions, the potential for error seems less likely than for other categories of admission. The occupational preferences require a job offer. Given their reliance on a particular employer, an immigrant will not likely move immediately after arriving in the U.S.[27] Such movement would be more likely among spousal admissions but still less than for other family-based admissions[28].

Finally, the census files record information for relatively few Indian and Filipino respondents. Although the data files contain appropriate weights to accommodate estimation, the files do not reproduce an exact count of Indians and Filipinos resident in each state.

---

[27] This type of movement may still occur, however. For example, an immigrant accepting a job in New York City may take up temporary residence in the city but then move to a suburb in New Jersey or Connecticut relatively soon after their arrival.

[28] When an immigrant gains admission through a spouse, the marital relationship involves a great deal of dependence between husband and wife such that the two most likely reside together. For an immigrant sponsored by a brother or sister, on the other hand, the same degree of dependence does not exist in most cases so the immigrant need not live anywhere close to their sponsor.

This weakness in the census files takes on special significance for states such as Idaho in which very few Indians and Filipinos reside[29].

Dependent and Independent Variables

In this chapter I attempt to assess the impact of state-specific resources on the residential decisions of recent immigrants. The analysis carries over from that conducted for the third chapter. As noted earlier, besides limiting the models to two admission categories (spousal and employment visas) and four occupations, I include only Indians and Filipinos. A simple state-specific count of the number of Indian and Filipino immigrants citing state *i* as their "state of intended residence" serves as the dependent variable at this stage of the research.

The models examine four state-specific independent variables with respect to their affect on the locational decisions of recent immigrants. The first construct indicates the average annual temperature of the state. Since most Indians and Filipinos arrive in the U.S. from warm climates, they most likely prefer those states with mild temperatures. Although unlikely to be the primary consideration among a majority of immigrants, I included it as a measure of the general environment facing immigrants to each state[30]. The second variable counts the number of fellow-natives resident in the state the year prior to the immigrant's admission. Although significance of this variable likely varies over time, the number of fellow natives in state *i* should exhibit a positive relationship to the number of immigrants selecting that state for settlement.

The last two independent variables account for employment opportunities in the state as they pertain to the immigrant's ethnic or

---

[29] One alternative to the PUMS files, the Current Population Survey, would overcome the problem of limited years for analysis since it is conducted both monthly and annually. However, use of the CPS would exacerbate the estimation problem due to its much smaller sample size (approximately 60,000 households).

[30] States such as California, due to their size, may exhibit very diverse intra-state average temperatures. However, the average annual temperature provides a sufficiently accurate measure of general conditions for the purposes of this analysis.

occupational group. The first of these variables indicates the median household income of fellow natives in state *i*.   Given the financial costs of immigrating and the quest for greater employment prospects in the United States, immigrants most likely choose those states which provide the greatest financial rewards for their service.   As such, median income should exhibit a positive relationship to the dependent variable.

The final variable represents the occupation-specific unemployment rates for each of the four occupations under consideration.   Given the extremely small numbers of Indians and Filipinos in a majority of the states, occupation-specific unemployment rates by nativity would suffer from unreliability.   The measure therefore identifies the unemployment rate for all physicians in state *i*, for example, without regard to ethnic origin.   Besides sample size considerations, using occupation-specific unemployment rates appears reasonable because immigrants compete for jobs with all similarly trained workers in the state, not simply fellow natives.   Since, by the regulations of the Department of Labor, immigrants may not take jobs from natives, conditions of high unemployment would lead to difficulties in job attainment for immigrants.   This variable should, therefore, vary negatively with the dependent variable.

Table 4-2 offers descriptive statistics of the data.   A number of significant differences emerge with respect to the two samples.   First, the percentages indicate that although the vast majority of both Indian and Filipino professionals admitted in 1982 and 1992 utilized employment visas, this was true to a greater extent for Indians (71% came through occupation-based visas compared with only 64% of Filipinos).   Not unexpectedly, males and engineers make up the bulk of the Indian sample while females and nurses vastly outnumber males and other professionals among Filipinos.   Finally, Filipino professionals immigrate to the U.S. at slightly later ages than do Indians, according to these data.   Differences in the samples will likely manifest themselves in the statistical results.

Table 4-2: Descriptive Statistics for Independent Variables

Variable	Indians	%	Filipinos	%	Total	%
Visa						
Spousal	429	28.8%	589	35.8%	1018	32.5%
Employment	1060	71.2%	1057	64.2%	2117	67.5%
Sex						
Males	921	61.9%	414	25.2%	1335	42.6%
Females	568	38.2%	1232	74.9%	1800	57.4%
Occupation						
Doctors	296	19.9%	144	8.8%	440	14.0%
Nurses	476	32.0%	1146	69.6%	1622	51.7%
Engineers	594	39.9%	302	18.4%	896	28.6%
Scientists	123	8.3%	54	3.3%	177	5.7%
Mean Age	33 Years		37 Years		35 Years	
Population	**1,489**		**1,646**		**3,135**	

Source: Immigration and Naturalization Service

Model Estimation

The analyses utilize Ordinary Least Squares (OLS) regression to study the impact of state-specific resources on the number of immigrants choosing a particular state as their area of intended residence. The models derive from the following basic equation:

$$\text{(Number of Immigrants Citing State, } i,\\ \text{as Area of Intended Residence)}\\ = Y_i = a_i + B_i X_i + e_i$$

where the X_i represents a matrix of the independent variables. The analysis incorporates five variations on the aforementioned model. The first model examines the impact of the state-specific factors on the number of immigrants entering each state while the second breaks the

**Table 4-3: Top Ten States of Residence Among Indian
and Filipino Physicians, Nurses, Engineers and Scientists,
1982 and 1992**

	Rank	1982 State	%	1992 State	%
Indians	1	New York	22.2	California	34.4
	2	Illinois	14.5	New York	11.5
	3	Texas	11.2	New Jersey	8.7
	4	California	10.9	Texas	6.7
	5	New Jersey	5.8	Illinois	5.4
	6	Pennsylvania	5.8	Maryland	4.5
	7	Massachusetts	3.0	Michigan	4.0
	8	Maryland	2.4	Pennsylvania	3.2
	9	Michigan	2.4	Virginia	2.6
	10	Florida	2.1	Florida	2.3
Total Pop.		*670*		*819*	
Filipinos	1	California	39.6	California	29.6
	2	Illinois	9.9	New Jersey	20.5
	3	New Jersey	5.2	New York	19.0
	4	New York	4.7	Texas	5.4
	5	Texas	4.1	Illinois	5.1
	6	Hawaii	3.9	Maryland	2.6
	7	Virginia	3.7	Florida	1.9
	8	Washington	3.7	Hawaii	1.9
	9	Michigan	3.2	Vermont	1.8
	10	Florida	3.0	Michigan	1.5
Total Pop.		*465*		*1,181*	

Source: Immigration and Naturalization Service

analysis down by year. Each subsequent model compares results across ethnic groups as well as across years to examine changes in the effects of the variables over time. The third, fourth and fifth models test for differences by occupation, visa class and sex, respectively.

As noted earlier, immigrant settlement often occurs in a concentrated manner. Table 4-1, from Barringer et al. (1993) showed the concentration in settlement of all Indians and all Filipinos in 1980 and 1990. A similar set of figures, derived from the data considered in this study, confirms the earlier patterns of settlement. Table 4-3 indicates the top ten states of residence for Indian and Filipino immigrants admitted as physicians, nurses, engineers and scientists in 1982 and 1992. As with the prior table, these numbers show that California, New York, New Jersey, Illinois, Hawaii and Texas represent the areas of residence for a disproportionate share of the immigrant populations in these groups. These facts lead to a tremendous skew in the distribution for the dependent variable. Most states take in a couple hundred Indian and Filipino immigrants on an annual basis but a few select states play host to thousands. These findings suggest that a more appropriate dependent variable would use the log to counteract the uneven distribution. However, analyses using the log of the original dependent variable did not alter the findings.

Results and Tests of Hypotheses
The results of the first regression analysis, reported in Table 4-4, appear to offer evidence in favor of the first hypothesis, but not overwhelmingly so. All of the variables except the occupation-specific unemployment rate exhibit the expected relationship to the dependent variable[31] and all attain significance in predicting the settlement patterns of Indian and Filipino immigrant professionals (with individual t-values significant at the 0.001 level or better). However, the significance measures do not clearly indicate which of the factors predominates.

Calculation of the coefficient of partial determination provides one means of determining the significance of individual predictors in a regression model. This modified measure, similar to the standard coefficient of multiple determination (R^2), indicates the marginal effect of adding an individual independent variable to the regression equation on reducing the variability associated with that model. Calculation of the coefficient requires comparison of the residual sum of squares of the equations with and without the variable of interest. The formula for

---

[31] The positive value on the coefficient for the unemployment rate may result from the fact that all of the professions exhibit generally low unemployment rates. This would actually indicate very favorable employment conditions for immigrants.

Table 4-4: Geographic and Economic Impacts on Choice of Residence

Variable	Coefficient	R^2_p
Median Income	0.0086**	0.2139
Unemployment	74.3241**	0.0590
Natives	0.5096**	0.1530
Average Temperature	0.7316	0.0007
Constant	-219.9892**	---
Overall F	DF (4, 3130) = 570.08	
R^2	0.4215	

** - Significant at the 0.01 level

Source: Immigration and Naturalization Service and U.S. Bureau of Census

an equation with four independent variables follows (Neter, Wasserman and Whitmore, 1993):

$$R^2_{Y4,321} = [SSR(X_1, X_2, X_3) - SSR(X_1, X_2, X_3, X_4)] / [SSR(X_1, X_2, X_3)]$$

The coefficient of partial determination (henceforth referenced as R^2_p), therefore, provides evidence of which factor, when added to an equation containing the remaining three independent variables under consideration, leads to the greatest reduction in residual variability. Although of less validity for assessing the contribution of a particular regressor to a subset of the variables of interest, the measure offers sufficient evidence for determining the role of a specific independent variable (Myers, 1990). The values of the partial R^2_p appear in the last column of Table 4-4.

The results indicate that median income and the presence of fellow natives most significantly reduce the error variability among the four variables included. The values reported favor median income over native communities as a predictor, with R^2_p values of 0.2139 and 0.1530, respectively. Interpretation of these results indicates that by including median income into a model that includes the other three variables, you reduce the residual variability by 21.39% while for fellow-natives, the reduction amounts to only 15.30%.

The lack of clear predominance with respect to employment-based economic conditions over the pull of fellow-natives may result from the fact that a large percentage of the immigrants in this sample (approximately 32%) gained admission through spousal visas. These immigrants more likely settle in areas of high co-ethnic concentration than do employment-based immigrants. In addition, if many of the occupational preference immigrants chose location based on the presence of occupational niches, then the existence of native communities could play a more important role than expected.

Important differences emerge both by nativity and year with respect to these findings. Incorporation of variables representing ethnicity and year into the previous model indicates highly significant values for both factors. Table 4-5 presents a model of the combined years which tests the significance of economic and other state-level indicators on the entry of Indians versus Filipinos. I present the models by year in the next section with respect to the second hypothesis. The hypothesis of the predominance of employment considerations receives much clearer support for Filipinos than for Indians. The findings for Filipinos more closely match the pattern exhibited in the pooled model with median income leading to near equal reductions in variability (at 33.6%) as native communities (33.9%). Among Indians, the presence of fellow-natives exerts the greatest influence on settlement patterns. Including the existence of fellow-native communities into the model for Indians led to a reduction in error variability of 71.3%; clearly, the most important factor of the four.

Among Filipinos, the existence of co-ethnic communities appears to play an important role in settlement decisions but less so than the potential earnings in the state of choice. Unemployment rates exert relatively less influence for both groups, most likely due to the low unemployment rates for these occupations in a vast majority of states[32]. The significance of average temperatures on the dependent variable

---

[32] Scientists in Alaska faced the highest unemployment rate (calculated at 14.85%) but in most cases the unemployment rate remained at around 2% for all four occupations and across all states. Scientists averaged the highest rates while physicians enjoyed practically full employment in every state.

**Table 4-5: Impact of Geographic and Economic
Conditions on Choice of Residence by Nativity Group**

Indians	Coefficient	R^2_p
Median Income	-0.0003	0.0009
Unemployment	28.09**	0.0331
Natives	7.89**	0.7732
Average Temperature	7.29**	0.1550
Constant	-503.99**	---
F	DF (4, 1484) = 2247.22	
R^2	0.8583	
Filipinos	**Coefficient**	R^2_p
Median Income	0.008**	0.3360
Unemployment	22.28**	0.0063
Natives	0.53**	0.3393
Average Temperature	-4.04**	0.0442
Constant	99.90**	---
F	DF (4, 1641) = 491.95	
R^2	0.5453	

** - Significant at the 0.01 level

Source: Immigration and Naturalization Service and U.S. Bureau of Census

suggests that other conditions in the state play an important, but much less significant, role in determining where immigrants choose to reside.

Breaking down the analysis by year in Table 4-6 demonstrates a clear and substantial reduction in the significance of ethnic communities on immigration patterns overall, but does not support the claim of overwhelming significance of employment factors in the 1990s. In the early 1980s, native communities played the greatest role in predicting immigrant settlement (with an R^2_p value of 0.8141). By the 1990s, median income increased in significance when compared to native communities but neither predominated as a factor. The level of occupation-specific unemployment also grew in significance over the period but to a much smaller extent. The general patterns observed for each year, however, appear to mask important differences across other individual characteristics. For example, a test for the significance of

Table 4-6: Impact of Geographic and Economic Conditions on Choice of Residence by Year

1982	Coefficient	R^2_p
Median Income	0.005**	0.0835
Unemployment	0.11	0.0000
Natives	1.21**	0.8141
Average Temperature	-1.04*	0.0182
Constant	10.60**	---
Overall F	DF (4, 1130) = 1336.27	
R^2	0.8255	
1992	**Coefficient**	R^2_p
Median Income	0.01**	0.1072
Unemployment	108.81**	0.0870
Natives	0.44**	0.1117
Average Temperature	0.37	0.0001
Constant	-333.25**	---
Overall F	DF (4, 1995) = 200.42	
R^2	0.2866	

* - Significant at the 0.05 level ** - Significant at the 0.01 level

Source: Immigration and Naturalization Service and U.S. Bureau of Census

immigrant ethnic background suggests important differences between Indians and Filipinos by year.

The findings pertaining to ethnic differences, reported in Table 4-7, indicate that in 1982 both Filipinos and Indians chose to settle in those areas with large co-ethnic populations (native communities reduced error variability by well over 90% for both groups). By 1992 the significance of co-ethnic as a predictor had declined among both groups and, for Filipinos, potential income became the dominant factor in determining immigrant location.

A second difference between the Indian and Filipino samples, besides the significance of individual predictors, emerges with respect to the generally poorer fit of the models among Filipino respondents in the 1990 sub-sample. The coefficient of determination (R^2) values reported in the ethnicity-specific tables suggest that some additional set of factors offer important information regarding the residential decision-making process of Filipinos in the 1990s. Whereas in 1982

Table 4-7: Predicting Choice of Residence: Ethnicity and Year

Indians	Variable	Coefficient	R^2_p
1982	Median Income	-0.007**	0.0106
	Unemployment	5.17**	0.0464
	Natives	5.40**	0.9524
	Average Temperature	1.78**	0.3409
	Constant	-85.06**	---
	F	DF (4, 665) = 3361.35	
	R^2	0.9529	
1992	Median Income	0.002*	0.0072
	Unemployment	38.32**	0.0439
	Natives	7.06**	0.7516
	Average Temperature	14.07**	0.2306
	Constant	-968.60**	---
	F	DF (4, 814) = 1060.95	
	R^2	0.8300	
Filipinos	**Variable**	**Coefficient**	R^2_p
1982	Median Income	0.008**	0.3677
	Unemployment	-8.004**	0.0171
	Natives	1.29**	0.9394
	Average Temperature	-1.87**	0.1265
	Constant	-16.70	---
	F	DF (4, 460) = 2086.40	
	R^2	0.9478	
1992	Median Income	0.02**	0.4255
	Unemployment	30.46**	0.0102
	Natives	0.52**	0.3827
	Average Temperature	-8.42**	0.1592
	Constant	-12.31	---
	F	DF (4, 1176) = 382.21	
	R^2	0.5652	

** - Significant at the 0.01 level

Source: Immigration and Naturalization Service and U.S. Bureau of Census

the four independent variables explained nearly 95% of the model's variation, by 1992 these same factors could explain only 57% of the variability.

The results prove somewhat difficult to interpret with respect to immigrant networking and run counter to expectations. If immigrants relied heavily on family sponsorship, as expected among Filipinos, immediately following the 1965 amendments then we would expect Filipinos to settle in areas with a large number of previous Filipino immigrants. Similarly, we should expect Indians to settle in a more dispersed manner based on their greater reliance on employment preferences. Among Filipinos, the results appear fairly consistent with expectations but the pattern observed for Indians do not follow from this logic; Indian settlement starts out as a process highly dependent on fellow-natives and remains so over the study period.

As discussed earlier, one explanation for these results could follow that Indians settle on the basis of ethnic occupational niches rather than simply ethnic niches. For example, if employers in the Silicon Valley hire predominantly Indian engineers, then you may see a clustering of recent Indian immigrants in California. Another possibility suggests that, by the 1980s, enough Indians had settled in the United States to provide the aid and resources to fellow-natives, which would encourage settlement centering on ethnic communities. Possibly, the sponsorship and settlement process occurs in a cyclical fashion and the patterns experienced by Filipinos soon after passage of the 1965 Amendments did not begin for Indians until some time in the late 1970s or early 1980s.

To confirm or refute the argument presented above would require additional information such as a longer time span for comparison (i.e., data from the INS and Census which would extend back to the 1960s and 1970s) or more specific information on residential decision-making at the neighborhood level. Unfortunately, such data do not exist at the present time. The issue warrants further study since it would contradict the following claim made by Portes (1987):

"Immigrant professionals and technicians do not tend to form concentrated ethnic communities but are usually dispersed throughout cities and regions and follow diverse career paths. More important, they generally enter the primary labor market, where they help to alleviate shortages in specific occupations" (p. 61)

Portes' argument may hold for the medical profession, for example, where foreign medical graduates often move to remote rural areas, inner-city hospitals or other areas shunned by native-born and U.S.-trained physicians. This logic may not hold for engineers or other occupations in which labor concentration could operate through ethnic niches. The results offer no evidence for concentration of settlement at the neighborhood or community level but suggest the need for further study.

Based on the preceding, it appears reasonable to next examine the influence of co-ethnics on settlement patterns by occupation and other relevant characteristics. The idea that ethnic niches might explain the continued significance of ethnic communities would receive some support if engineers rely more heavily on co-ethnics than physicians. The results of this analysis appear in Tables 4-8a for Indians and 4-8b for Filipinos. The findings offer some evidence in favor of the argument presented above. Among Indians, ethnic communities play the most important role in settlement patterns across all occupations in both 1982 and 1992 (with $R^2{}_p$ values of 0.9500 or larger for all professionals in 1982 and at greater than 60% in 1992). These results hold true more for engineers and scientists than for physicians and nurses in 1992. The $R^2{}_p$ values were calculated to be around 83% for engineers and scientists and close to 60% among physicians and nurses.

Ethnic communities played an important role among Filipinos as well in 1982, but the median household income of fellow natives had gained in significance by 1992 and barely surpassed the effect of fellow-natives among nurses. As in the case with Indians, native communities retain greatest significance among engineers between the two study years and least significance for physicians. The results for nurses and scientists carry the most interest in this case, however. In 1982 Filipino nurses apparently relied very heavily on fellow Filipinos to provide resources for settlement and adaptation. A possible scenario would suggest that hospitals recruited Filipino nurses in the 1980s who, in turn, found jobs for their friends from the Philippines. A number of

Table 4-8a: Impact of Geographic and Economic Conditions on Choice of Residence by Occupation, Indians

1982	DOC	NUR	ENG	SCI
Median Income	0.0002	-0.001**	-0.001**	0.001*
R^2_p	0.0010	0.0321	0.0506	0.0407
Unemployment	2.06	19.89**	-18.59**	0.46
R^2_p	0.0023	0.3660	0.2328	0.0013
Natives	5.53**	5.26**	5.63**	5.59**
R^2_p	0.9719	0.9528	0.9649	0.9663
Average Temp.	1.78**	1.51**	0.99**	1.16**
R^2_p	0.3748	0.3016	0.1648	0.2065
Constant	-103.46**	-71.67**	-1.59	-96.07**
F	**990.57**	**1831.40**	**1243.64**	**322.91**
DF	**(4, 107)**	**(4, 339)**	**(4, 167)**	**(4, 37)**
R^2	**0.9737**	**0.9558**	**0.9675**	**0.9722**
1992	**DOC**	**NUR**	**ENG**	**SCI**
Median Income	0.00006	0.003	0.001	-0.003
R^2_p	0.0000	0.0110	0.0080	0.0103
Unemployment	-220.91	-130.26**	-16.33	42.85
R^2_p	0.0607	0.0344	0.0048	0.2377
Natives	6.25**	6.12**	8.07**	7.82**
R^2_p	0.6061	0.6424	0.8265	0.8303
Average Temp.	11.77**	16.92**	11.19**	10.59**
R^2_p	0.2016	0.3311	0.1641	0.1442
Constant	-562.29**	-985.05**	-701.06**	-594.50**
F	**102.82**	**76.60**	**873.51**	**147.40**
DF	**(4, 179)**	**(4, 127)**	**(4, 417)**	**(4, 76)**
R^2	**0.6967**	**0.7070**	**0.8934**	**0.8858**

* - Significant at the 0.05 level ** - Significant at the 0.01 level

Source: Immigration and Naturalization Service and U.S. Bureau of Census

Table 4-8b: Impact of Geographic and Economic Conditions on Choice of Residence by Occupation, Filipinos

1982	DOC	NUR	ENG	SCI
Median Income	0.006**	0.006**	0.006**	0.009**
R^2_p	0.1430	0.1563	0.2773	0.2009
Unemployment	101.95	-45.83**	25.73**	0.74
R^2_p	0.2475	0.2233	0.0647	0.0003
Natives	1.26**	1.33**	1.31**	1.30**
R^2_p	0.9399	0.9392	0.9530	0.9291
Average Temp.	-3.09**	-1.67**	-2.09**	-2.84
R^2_p	0.1422	0.0715	0.1978	0.1400
Constant	44.40	69.37	-25.49	-7.68
F	221.02	1256.80	878.84	86.75
DF	(4, 44)	(4, 250)	(4, 130)	(4, 21)
R^2	0.9526	0.9526	0.9643	0.9429

1992	DOC	NUR	ENG	SCI
Median Income	0.009**	0.02**	0.008**	0.02**
R^2_p	0.2045	0.3940	0.2075	0.3485
Unemployment	496.39**	139.04	154.53**	52.00
R^2_p	0.2532	0.0332	0.3308	0.0757
Natives	0.52**	0.53**	0.53**	0.62**
R^2_p	0.4349	0.3498	0.6156	0.6331
Average Temp.	-8.85**	-9.63**	-8.41**	-1.42
R^2_p	0.1637	0.1455	0.3640	0.0081
Constant	0.66	-54.26	-52.13	-625.61
F	62.03	242.95	212.54	17.61
DF	(4, 90)	(4, 886)	(4, 162)	(4, 23)
R^2	0.7338	0.5231	0.8399	0.7539

** - Significant at the 0.01 level

Source: Immigration and Naturalization Service and U.S. Bureau of Census

studies observed patterns of nativity-specific hiring in the nursing profession which would support this pattern of settlement (Ong and Azores, 1994; Bashi, 1997).

By 1992, nursing recruitment may have become more entrenched throughout the country, especially given the introduction of special legislation relaxing immigration policies against foreign-trained nurses in the late 1980s. With more formalized recruitment procedures, Filipino nurses hoping to immigrate to the United States became less reliant on recommendations from previous immigrants.

Table 4-9 presents the findings by visa category at admission. One would expect that those individuals entering through spousal preferences would depend more heavily on ethnic communities, particularly if we assume shared nativity between the immigrant and his or her spouse. On the other hand, presence of a spouse may mean that the recent immigrant relies less on an extensive co-ethnic community for socialization and cultural adaptation. Newly arriving occupation-based immigrants, especially if they enter without family, may depend more heavily on fellow-natives for social resources.

The results suggest some support for the latter explanation among Indians. Although fellow-natives exert the strongest influence on settlement patterns among both spousal and employment admissions, those entering through employment sponsorship appear to depend on natives to a greater extent than do spousal entrants in the 1990s. The influence of this variable declines significantly from 1982 to 1992 but remains the most important predictor among Indian immigrants. To determine the reason for the continued significance of fellow-natives over employment prospects among employer-sponsored Indians would require comparison of the results for those entering with and without dependents, such as spouses and children. Unfortunately, the INS files do not record this type of data on their individual records.

Among Filipinos, native communities played as significant a role in the settlement patterns across visa categories as they did for Indians in 1982 but this factor declined in significance by a large margin over the study period. In the case of those individuals entering through spousal sponsorship, presence of natives remained the most important predictor of locational decision-making but median income gained in

Table 4-9: Impact of Geographic and Economic Conditions on Choice of Residence by Entry Visa, Indians and Filipinos

Indians	1982		1992	
	Spouse	Employer	Spouse	Employer
Median Income	-0.00002	-0.0008**	0.003*	0.0006
R^2_p	0.0000	0.0139	0.0126	0.0014
Unemployment	2.22	6.41**	-9.04	40.02**
R^2_p	0.0345	0.0025	0.0025	0.0492
Natives	5.58**	5.37**	5.81**	7.87**
R^2_p	0.9763	0.9482	0.6320	0.8447
Average Temp.	1.46**	1.79**	16.19**	7.69**
R^2_p	0.3269	0.3319	0.2990	0.0962
Constant	-84.66**	-83.44**	-1060.82**	-564.55**
F	**810.98**	**2716.15**	**224.50**	**1025.79**
DF	**(4, 76)**	**(4, 584)**	**(4, 343)**	**(4, 466)**
R^2	**0.9771**	**0.9490**	**0.7236**	**0.8980**
Filipinos	**Spouse**	**Employer**	**Spouse**	**Employer**
Median Income	0.008**	0.007**	0.01**	0.01**
R^2_p	0.3944	0.3596	0.3421	0.3333
Unemployment	2.89	-21.87**	28.99**	35.08**
R^2_p	0.0023	0.1346	0.0300	0.0079
Natives	1.32**	1.25**	0.67**	0.49**
R^2_p	0.9511	0.9327	0.6950	0.2777
Average Temp.	-2.78**	-0.17	-7.04**	-7.77**
R^2_p	0.2880	0.0010	0.2509	0.0775
Constant	5.83	-67.47**	-13.32	-4.80
F	**1486.41**	**850.86**	**320.39**	**184.31**
DF	**(4, 257)**	**(4, 198)**	**(4, 322)**	**(4, 849)**
R^2	**0.9586**	**0.9450**	**0.7992**	**0.4648**

* - Significant at the 0.05 level ** - Significant at the 0.01 level

Source: Immigration and Naturalization Service and U.S. Bureau of Census

significance by 1992. On the other hand, economic considerations became more important for employment entries by 1992, with the significance of native communities dropping dramatically to a value of 0.2777.

Finally, with respect to individual characteristics, Table 4-10 reports the findings by immigrant sex. As in the earlier tables, fellow natives prove the most important determinant of residential decisions in 1982 for both sending countries, with similar results for males and females. Although this factor declines in significance across all groups by 1992 some important differences emerge. First, natives continue to predominate as a factor in settlement among Indians, with men more heavily influenced than women. Given the evidence reported in the previous tables and the predominance of males in the engineering profession there appears further reason to suspect that immigrant settlement occurs in a more clustered pattern among engineers than among other professionals in the Indian community. A separate analysis at the neighborhood or community level would offer the evidence necessary to settle this question more firmly. In the case of Filipinos, the effect of co-ethnics declined more precipitously and economic factors became more influential. Among Filipinas, median income slightly edged out natives as the most important predictor of area of residence in 1992.

Comparing the results in Tables 4-8a, 4-8b and 4-10 demonstrate the interaction between occupation and immigrant sex. The two groups of professionals predominating in these analyses are Indian male engineers and Filipina nurses. The results for Indian engineers closely match those for Indian men while the numbers reported for Filipino nurses are practically identical to those for Filipinas. A more in-depth analysis would attempt to disentangle these effects and identify more relevant predictors, but these objectives are beyond the scope of this preliminary examination so they are deferred for future study.

Table 4-10: Impact of Geographic and Economic Conditions on Choice of Residence by Sex, Indians and Filipinos

Indians	1982		1992	
	Males	Females	Males	Females
Median Income	-0.0003	-0.001**	0.001	0.005*
R^2_p	0.0026	0.0309	0.0027	0.0278
Unemployment	-2.26*	18.05**	22.57	5.91**
R^2_p	0.0145	0.3281	0.0179	0.0006
Natives	5.47**	5.28**	7.50**	6.16**
R^2_p	0.9644	0.9532	0.7909	0.6595
Average Temp.	1.52**	1.59**	11.26**	17.97**
R^2_p	0.2956	0.3316	0.1657	0.3466
Constant	-74.00**	-74.88**	-741.68**	-1292.63**
F	**2025.23**	**1952.43**	**1017.26**	**134.91**
DF	**(4, 299)**	**(4, 361)**	**(4, 612)**	**(4, 197)**
R^2	**0.9644**	**0.9558**	**0.8693**	**0.7326**
Filipinos	**Males**	**Females**	**Males**	**Females**
Median Income	0.08**	0.007**	0.01**	0.01**
R^2_p	0.4041	0.2040	0.4188	0.3943
Unemployment	7.06	-14.11**	34.57**	74.38**
R^2_p	0.0117	0.0492	0.0339	0.0244
Natives	1.30**	1.29**	0.59**	0.52**
R^2_p	0.9467	0.9277	0.5360	0.3566
Average Temp.	-2.24**	-1.78**	-8.66**	-8.76**
R^2_p	0.2079	0.0637	0.2614	0.1363
Constant	-19.98	-0.87	-29.96	-18.37
F	**954.08**	**1170.24**	**145.91**	**265.46**
DF	**(4, 162)**	**(4, 293)**	**(4, 242)**	**(4, 929)**
R^2	**0.9593**	**0.9411**	**0.7069**	**0.5334**

* - Significant at the 0.05 level   ** - Significant at the 0.01 level

Source: Immigration and Naturalization Service and U.S. Bureau of Census

DISCUSSION AND CONCLUSIONS

This chapter sought to identify which resources in the destination area play the greatest role in determining where immigrant professionals initially decide to settle. Resources, which include the information and aid available in both the sending and receiving societies, represent one of the four basic elements of networks addressed in the second chapter. At this stage of the study, emphasis centered on conditions in the receiving country and how they determine patterns of settlement across the U.S. These issues prove important since, as Grieco (1998) noted, greater ethnic concentration in immigrant settlement patterns may lead to isolated immigrant communities which could, in turn, affect adaptation to the host society.

For comparison purposes, the analysis focused on two sending countries: India and the Philippines, and four occupations: physicians, nurses, engineers and scientists. These choices reflect the substantial numbers of foreign-born persons admitted under these occupational categories and the high representation of Indians and Filipinos in these groups. The chapter examined the impact of occupation-specific unemployment rates, ethnic-specific population sizes and income levels, and average state temperatures on the number of immigrants choosing a particular state as their area of intended residence in 1982 and 1992.

The results indicate that in the early 1980s, the presence of native communities had a significant impact on the settlement decisions of recent immigrants but that employment prospects (in the form of potential income) became increasingly important in the early 1990s. These findings appeared more true for Filipinos than for Indians, however, with the latter more reliant on co-ethnics for aid in residential decision-making. Finally, in addition to differences by ethnic groups, the regression results suggest important distinctions in the role of resources by occupation, admission class and immigrant sex as it interacts with occupation.

An earlier study (Vasegh-Daneshvary et al., 1986), conducted using the 1980 PUMS files, obtained similar results when examining Asians as a cohesive group. These authors found that the existence of Asian communities proved important to the settlement patterns of Asian immigrants but that employment opportunities (in that study state-specific unemployment rates, spending on research and development and the number of scientists) actually had greater effects than did co-ethnics. The results of this analysis confirm these findings but only among Filipinos and not until the 1990s. The discrepancies likely originate from the more specific approach taken in this analysis. Not only does this chapter focus on specific Asian groups but it also uses ethnic-specific employment measures.

I offered several explanations to account for the finding that ethnic communities played, initially, such an important role in the settlement patterns of immigrants and remained significant in a later period. One explanation suggests that professionals choose their initial state of residence as part of the development of ethnic niches in particular occupations. Patterns of nativity-specific recruitment and hiring occur within the nursing profession and may exist within the field of engineering as well. This could occur if formalized channels of recruitment operate internationally to bring in individuals wishing to enter the U.S. If this explanation holds then professionals may settle in areas of ethnic- and occupation-specific concentration with less concern for general employment prospects.

A second explanation attempts to account for the differences observed between Indians and Filipinos. Past studies suggested that Indians relied more on employment sponsors to gain entry to the U.S. immediately following the passage of the 1965 Amendments due to the small numbers of Indians resident in the U.S. at that time and the subsequent lack of sufficient potential family sponsors. Filipinos, on the other hand, had a larger pool of possible family and employment sponsors from which to choose. The importance of co-ethnic communities stems not only from their significance as immigrant sponsors, however, but also as sources of aid and support. Possibly, settlement patterns follow a cycle as ethnic communities develop. As a community becomes more established, reliance on co-ethnics increases (e.g., fellow-natives may offer more precise information in a more efficient manner than governmental or other formalized information sources) but once the size of the ethnic population reaches a critical level, that reliance decreases. Filipinos may simply be further advanced in this cycle than Indians due to their longer tenure in the U.S.

The findings have important implications for the use of networks among professionals. First, the data indicate which resources sustain professionals' migration, however, they do not provide the necessary evidence for determining how professionals utilize those resources in practice. The research may suggest important influences from co-ethnics but cannot adequately answer the question of exactly what type of aid they provide to immigrants. A better understanding of these effects would offer insights into how immigrants may successfully adapt to their host society. In addition, based on these data, we have no way to tell at which point in the immigration decision-making process these resources become useful. Since employment-based immigrants must obtain a job offer prior to their arrival, the influence must come at the recruitment stage but the same need not hold for spousal entries. Understanding the chronological development and use of resources would provide important evidence of network development.

The findings suggest, overwhelmingly, a need for further inquiry into the topic of resource development and utilization in network development and in the immigration process. In particular, the results indicate a need for further research at the individual level to determine how and when in the immigration process professionals use the resources available to them. Additionally, the findings call into question how individual circumstances (i.e., occupation, admission status, etc.) lead to differences in resource use and how resources affect immigrant adaptation. Specifically, researchers must find a way to address the question of whether professionals actually settle in concentrated communities, since previous work suggests this does not occur. Many of these questions require study through personal surveys since the existing national level data sets do not contain the relevant information to adequately address these issues. The next chapter offers some insight regarding resources through its use of personal interviews with immigrant professionals. However, the small sample sizes employed in the research reported in Chapter 5 suggest the need for follow-up using more in-depth techniques.

CHAPTER 5
Pilot Study of Immigrant Professionals in New York

INTRODUCTION
Networks and professionals
Analyses conducted in prior chapters offer support for the idea that professionals, like other immigrants, utilize networks during the immigration process. The data also suggest meaningful differences in the form and content of these networks over time and across a variety of individual characteristics. Finally, evidence suggests that weak ties play a very decisive role in the migration experiences of professionals who choose to come to the United States.

The previous chapters outlined a number of discoveries. First, using admissions categories to operationalize the primary forms of networks (i.e., strong- versus weak-ties) suggests that legislative decisions taken between 1972 and 1996 altered the availability and use of networks among professionals. The same set of analyses indicated significant differences in the use of networks by sex and occupation. Second, the resources available in the country of destination play an important role in determining settlement patterns of migrants and may change in significance over time. When a migration stream first develops, the presence of co-ethnics plays the greatest role in determining where immigrants choose to reside. Over time, this effect declines in significance compared to the employment opportunities prevalent in particular areas. The analyses also suggest very important differences by nationality with co-ethnics remaining more significant among Indian than among Filipino immigrants. Third, taken as a whole, the findings suggest that professionals utilize complex networks and that the networks professionals use differ considerably from the predominantly strong tie networks emphasized in many studies. Finally, the evidence suggests that professionals rely heavily on the structural conditions in existence at the particular time they choose to immigrate and in the sending and receiving societies. These conclusions support the findings from several recent studies of immigrant networking and offer further evidence of the need for subsequent research into patterns and forms of network development.

Gaps in Knowledge

The previous analyses still, however, leave many questions unanswered, leading to prominent gaps in our understanding of how professionals' networks develop and operate. Information available from the national data sets provide no means of addressing more specific questions regarding the immigration process. For example, what factors prompt professionals to consider migration in the first place? How do professionals locate appropriate contacts to aid in the immigration process (particularly in the case of employer sponsorship)? Is sponsorship, in fact, indicative of the type of network (i.e., strong or weak) utilized? In the case of weak-tie networks, how enduring are the ties? What role do norms play in the operation of migrant networks among professionals?

Purpose of Chapter

This chapter attempts to fill in some of these gaps through interviews with professionals in the New York metropolitan area. The work in this chapter represents a pilot study into the topics of interest and begins with a discussion of immigration experiences and network usage among five focus group participants. The final part of the analysis involves interviews with Indian and Filipino immigrants employed in one of the four occupations emphasized throughout this research (i.e., nurses, physicians, engineers and scientists) and working in the New York City metropolitan area. The chapter examines all four aspects of networks identified in Chapter 2 (i.e., structure, longitudinal factors, resources and norms) and provides the first insights, in this study, on the operation of norms in the immigration process.

This chapter limits data collection to first-level contacts with no attempt to map an entire migrant network. Implementation of social network analysis often calls for probing of second- and third-order contacts as a method of identifying specific elements of network structure. However, the resources available at this point did not permit a more in-depth analysis. Given the preliminary nature of the research for this chapter, I intend to provide some insights into the basic processes in operation and suggest ways to utilize the knowledge gained for a more extensive study.

The analysis will attempt to answer the following set of questions:

1) What structural forms do immigrant professionals' networks take?
2) Are there differences in network usage by sex, nativity and occupation?
3) Do resources play an important role in the immigration process?
4) Do professionals face strong normative pressures to aid family, friends and fellow-natives in further immigration?
5) Do professionals utilize enduring social ties or simply "action sets[33]"?
6) Do the ties of occupational immigrants encourage further immigration?

BACKGROUND
Prior Studies of Migrant Networks
Several recent studies addressed various aspects of network building and network operation across a variety of sending areas. Most of these studies relied on qualitative research methods including participant observation and ethnographic interviewing techniques. In most cases data collection occurred over an extended period of time and emphasized one or two aspects of migrant networks (e.g., structure and resources or longitudinal changes). Four, in particular, offer important insights into network operation for the purposes of this chapter.

Bashi (1997) examined the structure of migrant networks among West Indians in the New York metropolitan area. Using snowball sampling and oral histories, she attempted to map significant components of two separate networks, relying on information gathered from both the sending and receiving areas[34]. The first network

---

[33] The term "action set," coined by Mayer (1966), describes "an aspect of a personal network isolated in terms of a specific short-term instrumentally-defined interactional content" (quoted in Mitchell, 1969: 39-40).

[34] Bashi did not attempt to map the entire networks of the two groups she studied but ended the interviews when additional discussions offered no "new" evidence of network features.

included 33 individuals and the second 31 immigrants. From her research, Bashi developed a model of network building which she called the "Hub and Spoke Model," as a more refined alternative to the usual conception of a migration chain. She found that, in the West Indian case, migration does not occur in a linear fashion with one individual causing the migration of another but as a system of interconnected ties centered on particular individuals in key households. The "hubs" represent those households to which immigrants go when they arrive in the United States, with the "hub householder" the primary source of information and assistance. The "spokes" include new entrants aided in the immigration process by the hub householder.

Bashi found that immigration typically involves two distinct processes: the act of immigrating and socioeconomic integration. In the hub and spoke framework, the hub householder plays a significant role in both stages. Very often, the hub householder decides who "deserves" the opportunity to immigrate (e.g., based on their intellectual or economic "potential") and subsequently decides to whom they will provide assistance. The hub households typically developed around immigrant pioneers who entered the United States through recruitment channels and, based on their tenure in the U.S., possessed the resources to overcome some of the obstacles to immigration, including labor market conditions and relatively inflexible immigration laws.

Bashi suggested that her "Hub and Spoke Model" provides only one of many potential conceptualizations of networks which may develop to assist in the immigration process. Several of her more general findings bear strongly on the analysis that follows. First, she found that networks assist new immigrants through three primary channels: legal aid, job finding and the provision of temporary housing. As shown below, these same resources play the greatest role in network development among professionals. Second, she discovered important gender differences in the provision of these resources. Most significantly, job clustering occurred more among women with most female respondents taking positions in a small number of "female occupations" such as domestic work and nursing and men experiencing dispersion in a variety of positions. Finally, she discovered a culture of reciprocity within the network whereby network participants felt compelled to offer assistance to new arrivals.

Several reasons suggest, however, that the hub and spoke model may not accurately depict the process of network development and usage among professionals. Most of the immigrants in Bashi's sample entered the U.S. through pre-migration ties with very few coming as "pioneers." Many of the individuals in her sample had, in fact, entered illegally and, therefore, depended heavily on the network for legal aid and social adjustment. For these reasons, most of the immigrants she spoke with worked in jobs requiring few skills and recruitment through the recommendation of "veteran immigrants." Immigrant professionals possess far more resources and opportunities for legal immigration, which could reduce their reliance on former migrants.

Menjivar's (1997) study of Salvadoran immigrants to the San Francisco area shares many design features with Bashi's study. Menjivar followed fifty men and women over a period of four years in an attempt to examine the social, political and economic conditions at the time of arrival and to determine their effect on immigrant adaptation. Like Bashi, Menjivar utilized open-ended interviews supplemented with follow-ups and additional ethnographic fieldwork.

Several of the findings of Menjivar's study mirror those for West Indians despite the emphasis on kinship networks over other potential network forms. First, Menjivar identified three factors as responsible for the success or failure of migrant networks, two of which bear close resemblance to those cited in Bashi's study. In addition to the role of immigration policies and labor market opportunities, Menjivar found that community organization plays a decisive role in network development. She discovered that, in general, if the material conditions within a community do not favor the provision of assistance (e.g., earlier migrants do not possess the financial resources to aid others) then networks may collapse. If, as sometimes occurs, the networks *can* be maintained, they do not serve a useful purpose with respect to either future immigration or social adaptation.

Second, this study concluded that the same two processes identified in Bashi's study underlie the immigration experiences of Salvadorans in San Francisco. Menjivar specifically noted a need to draw a distinction between "networks [that act] as catalysts for migration and as facilitators in the resettlement process" (p. 120). Both authors, therefore, see different roles for networks in the process of actual movement and in subsequent adaptation to the host society.

Finally, and most significantly to the present chapter, Menjivar found that "... as the importance of kinship networks diminished, networks based on other social relations gained in prominence" (p. 106). This supports the idea that migrant networks do not exist as uni-dimensional entities but as complex structures incorporating a vast number of social relations at various stages of the immigration process. Ties to sponsors, for example, offer no guarantee of successfully finding a job (assuming immigration does not occur through employment preferences) or locating housing.

Hagan (1998) suggested that in addition to studying how networks operate at various stages of the immigration process (e.g., the decision to migrate, the direction of flows, transnational links and patterns of settlement), research should emphasize how networks change over time. Her three-year ethnographic study examined the experiences of the undocumented Mayan community in Houston. She also utilized participant observation and qualitative interviews in Houston and Guatemala to document longitudinal changes in the networks of 74 individuals.

As in Bashi's study, Hagan found distinct gender differences in the operation of networks over time, with women confined to one or two occupations and men employed in a variety of positions. Hagan contributed these distinctions to differences in the strength of ties predominating in men's and women's networks. All of the individuals in Hagan's study entered the U.S. illegally such that the labor market conditions they encountered on arrival led to greater dependence on a system of underground recruitment. Women typically found positions as domestics and became so heavily reliant on their employers for settlement assistance that their social and ethnic-based network ties broke down. Men, on the other hand, found jobs as laborers in a variety of settings and developed weak ties to more established immigrants and native-born persons.

Hagan's study, while less concerned with the larger structure of networks, documents the potential significance of the strength of ties to various aspects of immigration. Strong ties often aided immigrants in their search for jobs, but the weak ties men established led to greater success in legalization and in other aspects of incorporation. The results of this analysis, therefore, suggest that "success" in the immigration process depends crucially on the development of a wide variety of ties. Ideally, these ties should manifest various degrees of "strength" to overcome the large number of obstacles facing immigrants (although Bashi's study indicates that these ties can become localized into a small sub-set of persons and households).

Finally, a study of Fiji's Indian population (Grieco, 1998) offers some perspective into how conditions in the sending and receiving societies interact with the strength of ties to encourage either the formation of isolated ethnic communities or greater assimilation into the host society. Grieco claimed that the "migration auspices" (i.e., "the social, economic, political and historic contexts within which migration begins and proceeds," p. 706) determine which type of migration occurs; where "migration type" refers to the predominant mode of entry (in this case indentured labor migration versus "free" migration). The migration type, in turn, determines which type of tie predominates within a migrant population. In Grieco's study, indentured labor systems encouraged migration from a large number of geographic areas within India and fostered weak social ties between Indians in Fiji and, subsequently, greater assimilation into the larger society. Free entry, on the other hand, led to the migration of a large number of individuals from a particular geographic location and to the emphasis on strong ties and a reformation of social relations from India within Fiji.

Like the previous studies, Grieco's study consisted of face-to-face, open-ended interviews over a one and one-half year period and included approximately 50 individuals. Grieco supplemented these data with additional ethnographic data in the form of participant observation and through the use of archival data. Like the three previous authors, Grieco found that a variety of factors influence network formation within the host society, including immigration policy and mode of incorporation or the structure of community relations.

The research to follow supports many of these findings although the methods of data collection and the populations studied differ. First, this study emphasizes the experiences of professionals in the United States and specifically focuses on four occupations. In all of the aforementioned studies, the immigrant populations studied consisted of less-skilled workers and a larger number of occupations. Second, the following research attempted to incorporate comparison into the study design by including two distinct immigrant populations: Indians and Filipinos. Case studies suffer from the drawback that the research findings do not apply to other populations. By studying two groups of immigrants, I attempted to increase the generalizability of the findings.

Third, although I supplemented the interviews with additional qualitative data, several distinctions emerge in the study designs. This study employed a considerably smaller sample size (26 respondents) and included individuals recruited through contacts with ethnic professional associations and snowball sampling. Unlike the previously cited works, the survey instrument utilized in this chapter included both open-ended and closed-ended questions. The structure of the questionnaire permitted relatively quick completion of the interviews (two months) and in less time per interview than more open-ended designs (with the interviews lasting anywhere from fifteen minutes to one hour). In addition, the survey design allowed for phone interviewing. Although not preferable, a majority of the respondents insisted on being interviewed by phone because they felt they did not have the time to spare for a face-to-face meeting.

Although the design employed for this study did not permit a detailed description of case-specific network operation, this was not the intention of the chapter. Rather, I sought to explore all four aspects of network development as emphasized throughout the study and to provide some sense of comparison between two sending regions. As Bashi pointed out, the case study may not be representative of broader social trends but can offer "social significance" and can aid in theory building. This stage of the study therefore sought to provide additional insights into the ideas presented in earlier chapters and offer groundwork for further research into the migrant networks of professionals.

Results Suggested from Past Chapters
I summarized the results from previous chapters briefly above but several points deserve greater emphasis. Chapter 3 dealt primarily with the structure and longitudinal aspects of professionals' networks. Structurally, the analysis revealed that both strong and weak ties (operationalized through spousal- and employment-based admissions, respectively) play prominent roles in the migration of professionals. However, the results also demonstrated that individual and legislative factors influence the structure of these networks. In some years, curtailment of employment preferences led to shifts towards more family-based networks.

Through personal interviews it will be possible to elaborate more fully on network structure. Previously, it was difficult to identify more than a few elements of the networks' structure (e.g., INS, Department of Labor, employer and immigrant in the case of employment-based networks). In this chapter it will be possible to identify information channels, sources of support in the decision-making process, and more precise modes of entry. The studies described in the previous sub-section suggest that a variety of ties should predominate at each stage of the immigration process with different individuals and institutions relevant in each phase of settlement.

Chapter 3 also dealt with the issue of longitudinal outcomes in network development. The analysis revealed important shifts in network usage over time in response to legislative measures. With individual-specific data it will be possible to discern more directly how immigrants dealt with the introduction of immigration legislation and the time lags they experienced between the decision to migrate and their actual move. More importantly, the retrospective questions in the survey will allow a detailed history of individual migration. Given their greater resources, professionals are typically a mobile population, often making several trips abroad and to various destination areas before finally settling in a particular country. The ties they develop in any previous trips abroad can affect the types of networks they use to come to the U.S. This is one issue the retrospective questions attempt to address.

Chapter 4 dealt with the impact of resources on migrant decision-making. The analyses suggested that immigrants rely on different resources depending on the type of network they utilize. Employment immigrants are more heavily influenced by employment conditions than on the socio-cultural environment in the destination area. The findings also suggest, however, that historical patterns of migration from a sending country and the structural constraints encountered by individuals in particular occupations significantly affect the reliance on resources. For example, if foreign-trained physicians must accept positions in areas shunned by U.S. trained physicians, then the choice of initial area of residence may depend more on employment prospects in an area than on the presence of a large co-ethnic community.

The flexibility of a questionnaire allows exploration of a greater variety of resources, including less tangible factors such as psychological support. It should be possible to determine which resources had the greatest impact on individual migrants and why. Finally, in the absence of an opportunity to collect data in the sending countries, the survey creates a forum for discussion of the resources available to migrants in both the sending and receiving countries. This will aid in distinguishing between push and pull influences and the structural factors creating them.

Finally, both Chapters 3 and 4 demonstrated important differences in network usage depending on individual characteristics such as sex, occupation and nativity. These findings support the results of the studies cited earlier, particularly with respect to gender. Although the small sample utilized in this stage of the research is more suggestive than evidential, it should offer some grounds for future research into differential network usage.

Results from Focus Group Research
As the first step in this stage of the research, I conducted a focus group with five individuals, all with advanced degrees in the sciences or engineering. The discussion, guided by a series of questions regarding individual immigration experiences and the use of networks, lasted one and one-half hours. The discussion focussed on the following topics: 1) personal experiences in the decision to emigrate; 2) obstacles faced and resources used in the immigration process; 3) the definition of a network and the types of networks which exist; 4) how networks aid in immigration and 5) the types of networks most useful in the short- and long-term.

The results suggest that immigration legislation and the presence of friends or relatives in the U.S. played important roles in respondents' decisions to immigrate but that the actual act of moving took place in a relatively independent manner. The respondents agreed that different types of networks exist for various stages of the immigration process with weak ties predominating in the development of job contacts and strong ties aiding most in patterns of adaptation. Finally, in addition to social resources and network contacts, these participants indicated that personal resources, such as age, proved useful during settlement.

The focus group served as a guide in developing the survey instrument used at a later stage of the research. Although I am unaware of previous studies of migrant networks utilizing focus groups for the exploration of questionnaire design, Morgan (1996) discussed the increased reliance on this combination of methods in a variety of applications. When used to inform the content of a survey questionnaire focus groups serve to "provide data on how the respondents themselves talk about the topics of the survey" (ibid., p. 134). I felt it important to explore these topics before writing my survey in order to develop a more meaningful instrument.

Krueger (1988) presented several characteristics of the standard focus group. According to this source, focus groups represent a form of qualitative data collection based on a focused discussion. The researcher must decide on the general topics of interest and then develop a set of five to ten open-ended questions for group discussion. The facilitator should ensure confidentiality and encourage participants to express opposing points of view. To promote more open discussion, Kreuger suggested that participants be as homogeneous as possible with respect to pre-determined standards[35] but that they be unknown to one another.[36] These factors encourage the development of group dynamics which foster relevant discussion and do not inhibit disclosure. Krueger further suggested that the group size vary between four and twelve participants (i.e., small enough to encourage participation but large enough to provide diversity in responses) and that the deliberation last for approximately 90 minutes.

The discussion organized for this research proceeded under a number of ground rules laid out at the beginning of the meeting. First, I emphasized that the participants' names would not appear in either the transcript of the discussion (all agreed to allow taping) or in any subsequent reports, in order to protect their privacy. I informed them that I intended to use the information gathered to develop a survey instrument for further research into immigrant networking. I stressed the voluntary nature of participation and suggested that they could refuse to speak about a topic if they felt it too personal (at no point did anyone refuse to participate, however). I encouraged them to respect the confidentiality of the other four participants and suggested that they

---

[35] These "standards" reflect factors which the researcher wishes to control. For example, in this study, educational credentials of at least a master's degree and immigrant status were required to adequately represent the population of interest.

[36] The focus group for this study included four participants employed in the same multinational company. Although the four knew each other, I did not feel their familiarity inhibited open discussion of the topics addressed.

could relate the experiences of other people they knew so long as they did not reveal any names. Finally, I emphasized that focus groups do not consist of right or wrong answers and that they should respectfully share conflicting viewpoints. The meeting went very smoothly with full participation and with all of the respondents expressing their approval with the conduct of the session.

Table 5-1 presents the basic background information for the five focus group participants. As the table shows, the participants represent a diverse cross-section of sending countries and individual immigration experiences. All of the participants possessed high educational qualifications (each holding at least a master's degree) and the group included an almost even division by sex. Three of the five individuals originally entered the U.S. through a student (F-1) visa (although one individual obtained an exchange visitor, J-1, visa) and adjusted to either a temporary work visa for specialty occupations (H-1B) or permanent resident status. One respondent entered the U.S. at age 17, accompanying his parents and did not know his original visa status. Overall, these patterns reflect typical migration paths for immigrant professionals.

The short Participant Survey (used to collect demographic information) and the Moderator's Guide appear in the Appendix as Exhibits 5-1 and 5-2, respectively. The results of the session support many pre-conceived notions of how the immigration process operates among professionals but also suggest alternative points for consideration.

Many of the findings pertain to network structure. All five participants had some contact with the U.S. prior to their decision to migrate. One woman came to the U.S. previously for work while the second female participant said that American professors in her home country encouraged her to consider migrating to the U.S. The remaining respondents knew either friends or family members in the U.S. before coming.

Several of the individuals, however, indicated that they had not necessarily intended to immigrate to the U.S. These respondents suggested that they entered the U.S. on a trial basis or simply to visit but either returned to the U.S. at a later date or simply found some way to remain. The Chinese participant (henceforth referenced as "S") said she had not intended, necessarily, to stay in the U.S.: "*... when I first*

Table 5-1: Descriptive Statistics of Focus Group Participants

Variable	Frequency
Sex	
Male	3
Female	2
Years Spent as Continuous Residents of the U.S.	
5-10	2
11-20	2
20+	1
Educational Background	
Master's	2
Ph.D.	3
Country of Birth	
Armenia	1
Austria	1
China	1
Ghana	1
India	1
Visa Status Upon Entry	
F1	3
J1	1
Unknown	1
Current Visa Status	
H-1B	2
Permanent Resident	2
United States Citizen	1
Total Participants	5

left China, I wasn't, I didn't expect to immigrate here. I was just planning to come here to study." A respondent from Ghana (J) echoed this sentiment saying, "*... for me it was more, probably like a bunch of ... incidents feeding off each other. I had never really planned to come here. It was just that I was in Canada and next door was here and so ...*" Finally, an Austrian woman (E) who had originally come to the U.S. in the mid 1970s but came back again after a couple of years added, "*I think there's a big difference for instance between the three of us* [herself, S and J] *and between* [H, an Armenian who had come to the U.S. "to escape the Soviet Union"] *because, for instance, you it was, for you* [H] *immigration was the goal. ... we weren't really, we hadn't* *really decided we wanted to immigrate at the time when we came, it was, 'Let's try it out and if we like it we'll see where it goes.'"*

These comments suggest a need for further inquiry into migration intentions and for a broader conception of immigration which treats the process as more continual in nature, without a set time frame. Professionals, in particular, (with greater resources at their disposal) may not see a move to the U.S as a conclusion to the immigration process. Even those with "settled" lives consider either returning to their home country or moving to some other place if better opportunities arise.

The discussion revealed that these professionals take for granted the fact that different networks exist to fulfill social and economic needs, as shown in the following exchange:

Researcher: So I, first of all, let's talk about what is a, a personal network?
A [Indian]*: You, you're talking about in the context of jobs, specifically, or ...?*
Researcher: So, what you're saying is that there are different types of networks depending on jobs, social ...?
E [Austrian]*: Well, sure.*
J [Ghanaian]*: Yeah.*
A: Yeah.

All of the respondents strongly supported the notion that different types of networks exist for different phases of the immigration process. For example, respondents used different contacts to enter the U.S. and to obtain employment. All of the respondents agreed that strong ties to fellow-natives played a role in each phase of network development but offered the greatest aid in terms of information exchanges, the establishment of social contacts and other aspects of settlement, as the following indicates:

A [Indian]*: ... you come here you don't know anybody, you don't have an apartment, you don't know how to look for an apartment, you don't have enough dollars - Indian currency's limited. You can have a certain, you have a hundred dollars, something like that, that's not enough to pay for the first month's half rent, so, ... you need a certain amount of support*

and you come in. I, uh, when I landed at the airport somebody was there to receive me, this was obviously an Indian guy, were two, there were two Indian guys. ...so, what I'm saying is that, initially, the first interaction is with Indians.
S [Chinese]: *It's similar with Chinese students too.*

With respect to job networks two respondents suggested that in the development of job networks, fellow-natives may show preference by asking more questions and offering more personal time than Americans or other potential contacts in the process of establishing career ties and exploring job prospects. Some excerpts follow:

A [Indian]: *... a job-related network becomes relevant to you it, it takes, firstly, it takes a while to form a job-related network. Because, by definition, since we are distinct, distinguishing between social and job-related, you did, you did not know these people earlier, before you started finding a job and that's how they became your job-related network people. So you, since you don't know them it takes a while to build that network. ...in terms of the job they would be, there would be other Indians who would be, who would probably be more willing to advise you .. than who are not Indian. Um, especially Indians with the same kind of background ... would be more willing to say things like, 'Okay, so you're looking for, you're not looking for an academic job, you're looking for an investment industry job. Why? Is the academic job market bad? How is the job market?' An Indian would be more willing to get into a conversation like that with you on the phone.*

H [Armenian]: *...my personal experience is you have the contacts after you've been in the industry for a couple of years.*
Researcher: Do you, would you favor other Armenians? If an Armenian came to you and needed help would you be more willing to help, to give that person more of your time? Or have you experienced other people, because you're Armenian ...?

H: ... The first, first impression, yes. I mean, you know 'cause it's, it's, you can't help it ...
Researcher: Well, also in looking for a job you may not have the capability yourself of getting someone a job but at least you can pass on information?
H: Oh yes I, I would. Yes, I would.

However, as noted earlier, these focus group participants originally entered the U.S. through either family or non-immigrant visas so their statements regarding the process of employment networking may not hold for those gaining admission through occupational preferences.

Finally, with respect to network structure, age appears to play a significant role in determining the degree to which immigrants rely on contacts. One respondent suggested that, socially, networks proved less important for him than for others because he entered the United States in his mid-20s when we was more focused on his studies than younger students.

A [Indian]: ... I was not as young as, uh, some of you. So, uh, the question of social interaction was not very important. Because, because I was never in such need of social interaction. When you're younger you're in greater need, when you're older you tend to interact in different ways. I think older people tend to interact in similar ways in different countries.

In discussing his personal experiences with discrimination, the participant from Ghana admitted difficulties in dealing with it at times but that it didn't inhibit his interaction in the long-term due to his age.

J [Ghanaian]: Socially it kind of sucked because I couldn't figure out what these people are about. ...it didn't bother me because for me, I wasn't proud. I was, it was like, 'Yeah, I knew what you guys were about. But mind you too, I was a little bit older than them because I, when I entered freshman year I was 19; a lot of them were like 16, 17.

A third participant who entered at a more advanced stage of her career clearly emphasized her independence in moving to the U.S., in establishing residence and in making a name for herself in her profession.

> *E* [Austrian]: *...I really did not know, in New York, anybody but the guy who had actually hired me. I didn't know a soul. I came here, there was me and the lab. And I really, I had to start from scratch too, with everything because the whole department started from scratch. So, I was without help or any knowledge of anybody else. ... No, when I came there was nobody at the airport to receive me. Uh, I came on December 28, 1982. They had, oh yeah, they wrote me a letter, they had an apartment for me in the Bronx hospital apartment, just across the street. I said, 'Great!" I came, there was nothing in this apartment was completely **empty**. There was no bed, there was no chair, there was no electricity, there was nothing and everybody [new co-workers] said, 'Happy New Year!' turned around and left.*

These findings suggest that more mature immigrants possess the resources necessary to immigrate without as much support from family and friends.

Some of the more interesting findings pertain to immigrant adaptation. First, as pointed out earlier, co-ethnics did provide some settlement support such as locating an apartment and aiding in initial rent payments. However, this type of assistance occurred more frequently among immigrants from larger U.S.-based communities (i.e., Indians and Chinese) than among smaller groups. In addition to the points made earlier, the Indian respondent shared the following:

> *A [Indian]: Indian contacts get thrown in your lap the moment you come in, especially in school because every school would have some kind of an Indian association ...*

The second important finding with respect to adaptation concerned the solidarity the respondents felt as a consequence of American attitudes towards them based on pre-conceived notions of their countries of birth. Several of the participants reported having to work especially hard to succeed and "prove themselves" to natives and at

least two of the respondents said they experienced discrimination, as
the following points show:

>   *E* [Austrian]: *I found some kind, I felt, discrimination in terms
>   of like, salary and difficulty in obtaining ... positions. I
>   thought it was very hard for me, maybe as a woman, maybe as
>   a foreigner, to get to the same level in my profession. Um, I
>   thought there was some kind of discrimination there.*
>   *Researcher: And how did you overcome that? Did you just
>   fight on ...*
>   *E: By effort. Just by effort and working hard. I mean, you
>   eventually you get to the same level. It just takes a bit longer.*

>   *S* [Chinese]: *... You know, uh, I first got to this country, when
>   I first got here I went to Iowa. ... People there, they are nice
>   people but, uh, you know they are not like people on the east
>   or west coast. Uh, they* [people on east and west coast] *are
>   more exposed to the outside world. So, those people* [people
>   in Iowa], *you know, they really don't know much about the
>   outside world, a lot of the students, you know - and they don't
>   care. They don't care about it, they don't want to know ...
>   about it. So, it's like, you get there, you're with these group of
>   Americans, all they cared is about America. They don't care,
>   they don't ask you questions about your country ... See, you
>   think, you see too many Asian students, the Americans,
>   sometimes they go to another class. They say, if it's a math
>   class or some, when they see so many Asian students in that
>   classroom they will switch to another.*
>   *A* [Indian]: *... I was in Iowa too. So, uh, Iowa, people in Iowa
>   don't have a notion of, by and large, I think it's true to say,
>   they don't have a notion of anything other than the U.S.
>   Probably anything other than ...*
>   *S: The Midwest.*
>   *A: ...Iowa City. Or Cedar Rapids, Iowa. You know, basically,
>   very, very local, uh, orientation. Uh, so to answer your
>   question, no, they don't know, uh, anything about India. But
>   they do, broad stereotypes develop. People do think Indians
>   are good with computers.*

The experiences related by J, from Ghana, indicated that he faced stereotypes of immigrants as well as strong racial biases, as is clear from the following sections of transcript:

J [Ghanaian]*: ... The, initially, I guess initially, it is, it was, the biggest thing, probably, initially it was harder to actually, uh get to build good friendships with people because I found out that everybody was so ignorant about where I was coming from. And, uh, I had to, I can't begin to tell you how many times I had to answer questions like, uh, 'Did you ever wear clothes before you came here?' or 'Do you guys live in trees like we see on television?' or 'Do you...' you know, '...hunt monkeys to eat?' That sort of stuff. So, at first it was, it's like, they'll ask things like, 'So, how did you get here?' or ask 'Did you swim across or what?' You know, 'Do they have airports where you're from ...?'*

H [Armenian]*: Is that, is that at MIT? Nah, no?*

J: That's MIT!

H: You're kidding!?!

*J: I'm telling you! ... So that was annoying ... you know, because everybody was so ignorant about you. Um, people, people were kinda standoffish. They, they initially they assume you are stupid, okay, because you're coming from Africa, what else could you know, right? So, they assume you're stupid. They wouldn't want to do anything academic with you. I used to do my homework by myself. Uh, **everything** to do with school I used to do by myself. Uh, I used to, when we're doing labs and you have to, like, pair up with people, I **always** had to be the person to go and ask somebody, 'Would you ...' you know, '... pair up with me?' Yeah, I had to do that, otherwise, you know, I wasn't going to get a partner and **grudgingly** so, somebody would say, 'Yeah, I can let you ...' So, so that was tough. ... it was interesting because, what happened was, um, one day, this is like, see freshman year at MIT you don't, they don't grade you, you're on pass-fail, right, you gotta pass your class or you fail your class. Uh, and then sophomore year they start to grade you, right. So, I think at the end of my sophomore year, one of the, this Chinese girl who lived on my floor - this was an American* *born - and she came to my room and she saw, I think I had my transcript on my desk and she saw it. She saw that I had all A's. And she was so surprised. I remember that. She was so startled. The **next day**, everybody on the floor knew that, you know, I was a straight A student. So, uh, a month later I started getting friends. You know, I started getting invited to do homeworks with people, you know. And, um, that's how I, sort of, uh, became quote-unquote accepted.*

These problems seemed to cause respondents to feel more positively about their country of birth[37].

Finally, two additional points bear mention. First, immigration policy clearly played an important role in the migration process for these immigrants, particularly in the case of the Armenian participant whose family benefited from generally open borders policies towards people fleeing communist countries.

H [Armenian]*: ... it took us, I think, about seven or eight years to get permission from the local government to leave. And at that time, America basically had an open door policy toward Communist countries, Iron Curtain countries, so it was very easy to get permission to, uh, to enter America and very hard to leave, um, Armenia - at that time part of the Soviet Union. So, so just after waiting for about seven years, you know, we left.*

Secondly, these immigrants cited a variety of factors as motivating their move to the U.S. from chance circumstances and general social pressure to do so, to better opportunities for advancement and a better way of life. While none of the participants entered through a family-based visa a couple of them did say that knowing others (either family

---

[37] These results run directly counter to a claim made by Cheng and Yang (1998). These authors claim that "The training [foreign students receive in the U.S.] ... weakens their traditionalist and nationalist values, especially when these are defined in advanced countries as 'backward'" (p. 633). The evidence from this small group actually suggests that prejudicial attitudes encourage individuals in these circumstances to feel greater pride in their home countries.

or friends) in the United States had a favorable impact on their decision to come here. Each person reported unique reasons.

E [Austrian]: *I started thinking about coming to the U.S. for two reasons. One was professional, I came from Austria. I wasn't too happy with my job at the University of Vienna. So, I wanted to come back after having been here a year earlier. I wanted to come back. The other reason was personal, because I had a boyfriend. ... [the boyfriend] was not as important as the professional. ... I had been in Denver, Colorado for a one-year postdoctoral fellowship 1976-1977. I really liked it very much. ... I like the way they were running their labs, being a biologist a new laboratory is essential to my job. ...It was much more focused and I really like the way, a reason was the funds here and see in 1982 Europe was still pretty far behind I mean, in my, in tumoral biology. France, Italy, Germany, Austria, they were not was much advanced as they are now. ... American was much more advanced. For me, this was the place to go. And that's that.*

S [Chinese]: *... I also wanted to come to the States to see how this country is and also to have some advanced education here, so I majored in English when I was in China. ... I like the fact that you have the freedom to do what you want to do here. ... one of the professors very, he was very nice and he always encouraged me to, to come to the States.*

J [Ghanaian]: *.. I was, like, getting to see another part of the world and I was gonna meet all these people, interesting people from all kinds, all types, right. ... 'Well, I'd seen Canada ... there's a country next door ...' you know, '...and I've heard a lot about it but I haven't been' so I decided that I was going to apply to colleges in the United States. So, then I decided to go to, to come to a university here because the choice was either I come here or I go to Ghana, right. And, I was still in that high of trying to discover places.*

H [Armenian]: *... Kruschev came to power in the Soviet Union. He decided to loosen emigration from, uh, the Soviet*

Union at that time. Basically, three groups started emigrating. They were pretty unhappy and they were actually had a lot of relatives and connections outside of Soviet Union: Armenians, Germans and Jews. ... So, so, why America? I mean, basically, it was personally you could enter easily and then you had relatives here.

A [Indian]: *... I went to a school where, where people tend to assume that, um, that either you go to the U.S. or you don't. Uh, by that, what I mean is that it's not considered abnormal to go to the U.S. It's kind of considered normal. It's a normal question that, if you went to that school, uh, which is, uh, IIT-Delhi, people would ask you, 'So, are you, when you graduate, are you going to the U.S. or not?' It's kind of a normal question to ask. ... So, uh, what I'm basically saying is that this thought process was always in my mind. Going to the U.S. or not going to the U.S. Uh, what tilted the balance in favor of my going to the U.S. was that my brother was here.*

The focus group session did, therefore, fill in some of the gaps in knowledge left by the analyses conducted for earlier chapters. Although based on the experiences of only five individuals, it helped in establishing a framework from which to devise a survey instrument to study various aspects of immigrant network building. The meeting suggested that professionals possess enough resources to undertake immigration independently, that weak ties predominate in a large number of circumstances but that strong ties can certainly perform essential functions and that immigrants' networks change, sometimes dramatically, over time and in response to the needs they encounter, first in trying to enter the U.S. and then in various stages of settlement and adaptation. These findings guided the research design into the second stage of the analysis for this chapter.

METHOD
Indians and Filipinos in the New York Area
Asia, in general, represents the third largest source area for foreign-born residents of New York City (the Caribbean and Europe send the first and second largest numbers, respectively). Among Asians in New York City, Chinese form the largest group followed by Indians and

Filipinos (Passell and Clark, 1998).   However, among the occupations considered in this research, Indians and Filipinos constitute two of the largest ethnic groups in the New York area (Barringer, Gardner and Levin, 1993).   As such, the survey for this section of the chapter focused on foreign-born Indian and Filipino professionals employed as either physicians, nurses, engineers or scientists in the New York metropolitan area.

The survey made no attempt at representativeness due to the insufficiency of time and financial resources.   Instead, the sample attempted to cover the most prominent native-occupational groups identified in Chapter 4.   Bivariate tabulations for Indians and Filipinos (based on the 1982 and 1992 INS data files and reported in Table 5-2) suggest that male engineers represented a majority of the Indians admitted (18.25%) while a similar percentage of Filipinos fell into the cell for female nurses (34.9%).

Further examination of the figures in Table 5-2 shows that certain sex-occupation categories represent uncommon combinations for Indians or Filipinos.   For example, very few Indian men enter the U.S. as nurses (only 0.38% of the sample).   Similarly, Filipino women do not generally enter as engineers (just 0.41% of the total).   The sampling for the survey therefore made no special attempt to locate respondents from either of these sex-occupation groups.   In all other cases, I made an attempt to locate at least two respondents from each of the other categories.   This led to a projected sample of twelve Indians and fourteen Filipinos.

I located potential respondents through contacts with various ethnic and occupation-specific professional associations in the New York City area including the Association of Indians in America's New York Chapter, the Philippine Nurses Association of New York and the Society of Filipino Engineers, among others[38].   Representatives from these organizations provided lists of potential contacts.   I then contacted every individual and requested their cooperation in a face-to-

---

[38] In the case of Filipinos, I relied to a greater extent on personal contacts.   In several cases, contact with a Filipino professional association resulted in phoning of an individual residence and in two of these cases I reached a retired, former member of the association who could not provide information for further potential interviewees.

Table 5-2: Distribution of Indians and Filipinos in New York City by Sex and Occupation, 1982 and 1992

Indians				
Occupation	Male		Female	
	Number	% of Sample	Number	% of Sample
Physicians	227	7.24%	69	2.20%
Nurses	12	0.38%	464	14.80%
Engineers	572	18.25%	22	0.70%
Scientists	110	3.51%	13	0.41%
Total	**921**	**29.38%**	**568**	**18.12%**
Filipinos				
Occupation	Male		Female	
	Number	% of Sample	Number	% of Sample
Physicians	57	1.82%	87	2.78%
Nurses	52	1.66%	1094	34.90%
Engineers	277	8.84%	25	0.80%
Scientists	28	0.89%	26	0.83%
Total	**414**	**13.21%**	**1232**	**39.30%**

Source: Immigration and Naturalization Service

face or telephone interview[39] at the respondents' convenience. In several cases, these contacts then provided names of friends, family members and co-workers who they thought might also agree to an interview which resulted in the use of some snowball sampling.

Types of Questions Asked
The survey instrument appears in the Appendix as Exhibit 5-3. The questionnaire included five distinct sections. First, I collected basic demographic data regarding the respondent's age, marital status, sex, educational background/training and birthplace. The remaining

---

[39] Originally, I intended to conduct all of the interviews face-to-face. However, this proved impossible. Given their professional responsibilities, long work hours and variable schedules, a majority of the respondents felt they did not have the time available to arrange a face-to-face meeting. Although unfortunate, given the potential for gaining additional contextual information through in-person interviews, I sacrificed these benefits in the interest of greater participation.

sections attempted to address each of the four general elements of networks identified in the second chapter. The second section of the questionnaire addressed the longitudinal migration histories of the respondents. It included the number of previous moves outside the respondent's country of birth, the reasons for moving, the visa status utilized during previous stays and relevant aspects of the most recent migration into the United States including current visa status. The third section examined network structure. I asked respondents to identify the individuals most influential to their decision to move with respect to advice, information, support and sponsorship. The fourth section considered network resources. It included questions relating to obtaining job information and placement, adaptive resources in the form of social support and the maintenance of ties to the respondent's country of birth. Finally, the fifth part of the survey examined norms relating to the immigration experience. The information requested included the sponsorship of relatives by the respondent, any likely future plans for sponsorship and forms of aid and assistance provided to others by the respondent.

RESULTS
Basic Findings
Tables 5-3 through 5-5 summarize some of the more important findings as gathered from the survey respondents. Table 5-3 presents basic background information on the respondents with respect to the demographic questions asked. As seen in the bottom row of the table, the samples do not reflect the intended sizes. Individuals contacted though the Indian associations provided a larger number of names for potential respondents than did members of the Filipino organizations. One reason for the lower cooperation of Filipinos was that the Filipino association members represented an older, and often retired, population who could not provide sufficient contacts. In addition, I could not locate enough physicians for the sample. Only three physicians, one Indian and two Filipinas, agreed to interviews. In three cases, the individual refused to participate citing a lack of time and too heavy a workload and in two other cases, I gave up trying to reach the potential respondent after over a dozen calls.

The samples do, however, accurately reflect the figures reported in Table 5-2 in that Indian male engineers and Filipina nurses made up the majority of the sample (28% and 20%, respectively). The occupational

Table 5-3: Demographic Characteristics of Survey Respondents

Variable	Indians	Filipinos
Sex		
Male	8	3
Female	6	8
Mean Age	33.9	50.1
Marital Status		
Never Married	0	2
Married	14	7
Widowed	0	1
Divorced	0	1
Education Completed		
Home Country	8	8
United States	6	3
Highest Degree Obtained		
Bachelor's	4	9
Master's	7	0
Ph.D. / M.D.	3	2
Occupation		
Physician	1	2
Nurse	0	5
Engineer	8	3
Scientist	5	1
Total Sample Size	14	11

distribution also largely explains why Indians had higher educational credentials than the Filipino respondents overall. Since most of the Filipinos reported nursing as their occupation and a large number of Indians worked as either scientists or physicians, the educational requirements were greater among the Indian respondents.

Significant age differences emerged between the two populations. The Indian respondents were, overall, much younger than the Filipinos in the sample (with average ages of 34 years for Indians and 50 among Filipinos). This largely reflects the differences in year of arrival among the respondents, a point I return to later. The difference in ages also reflects the large number of Indian women who arrived relatively soon after marriage. Cultural preferences favoring a 3 to 5 year age gap between husbands and wives in India (with the husband the older of the two) and generally younger ages at marriage (when compared to the average age of marriage in the United States) suggest that Indian women who arrive soon after marriage enter at relatively young ages.

In general, the results with respect to respondent ages conform to expectations regarding the arrival of immigrant professionals. Most studies of professionals indicate that they migrate at later ages than less-skilled workers in part due to the training required for their professions and also due to the greater distances traveled by a majority of these immigrants. Longer distance travel generally requires greater savings, which usually takes time to accumulate in "Third World" countries. For these reasons, it also comes as no surprise to find that most of the respondents (and all of the Indians) were married.

Finally, most of the survey respondents completed their education before arriving in the United States. Among Indians, nearly equal numbers of respondents finished their schooling in the United States and India. Among Filipinos, on the other hand, several of the respondents completed their education in the U.S. but twice as many earned their degrees before their arrival. None of the respondents obtained degrees from other foreign universities. These results suggest the importance of educational opportunities as a motivation for immigration for professionals.

Table 5-4 presents some of the preliminary findings with respect to the immigration histories of the respondents. In general, the Filipino respondents arrived in the U.S. earlier than the Indians. Most of the Indians in the sample came to the U.S. sometime after the 1990 Immigration Act passed while many of the Filipinos arrived in either the late 1970s or early 1980s. Although four Filipinos arrived in the U.S. prior to 1975, none of the Indians did so. These results also match general expectations in the sense that Filipinos began arriving in the U.S. in large numbers soon after passage of the 1965 amendments to the Immigration Act.

A vast majority of the respondents had never been to the United States before their decision to settle here but two individuals had come many times for business (both claiming to have been in the U.S. at least fifty times before immigrating!). Most of the respondents came directly to the U.S. from their country of birth. However, among those reporting having lived in a third country for some time, the reasons differed between Indian and Filipino respondents. The three Indians

Table 5-4: Immigration Histories of Survey Respondents

Variable		Indians	Filipinos
Year of Settlement	1965 or Earlier	0	1
	1966-1975	0	3
	1976-1988	2	5
	1989-1991	4	1
	1992 or Later	8	1
Average Years in U.S.		5	19.8
Average Age When Came to the U.S.		28.9	30.3
Prior Country of Residence	Home Country	11	8
	Other Country	3	3
Number of Previous Trips	None	10	7
	1-3	3	3
	4+	1	1
Visa Status Upon Arrival	Family	0	1
	Employment	0	3
	F1	4	1
	H-1A	0	2
	H-1B	3	0
	J1	0	0
	Other	7	4
Current Visa Status	Citizen	0	9
	Permanent	8	1
	J-1	0	0
	H-1A	0	0
	H-1B	5	0
	Other	1	1
Reasons for Moving to U.S.	Political	0	1
	Education	4	1
	Employment	9	9
	Join Family	6	3
	To See U.S.	2	2
State of Residence at Arrival	New York	1	4
	New Jersey	0	4
	Connecticut	3	0
	Other	10	3
Total Sample Size		**14**	**11**

Table 5-5: Aspects of Immigrant Networks Among Respondents

Variable		Indians		Filipinos	
		Men	Women	Men	Women
Time to Adjustment	Non-Immigrant	5	1	0	1
	0-3 Years	2	5	0	1
	4-5 Years	0	0	1	0
	6+ Years	1	0	2	6
Intend to Move Back	No	3	1	1	2
	Yes	1	0	1	1
	Maybe	4	5	1	5
Original Visa Status	Principal	8	1	2	8
	Dependent	0	5	1	0
Involved in Decision	Parents/Family	5	2	1	3
	Friends	1	1	0	0
	Recruiter	0	0	1	0
	No One	2	3	1	4
	Others	0	0	0	1
Use of Resources	Family Only	3	3	1	1
	Employer Only	1	0	0	1
	Both	4	3	2	6
Information Source	Transfer	3	0	0	1
	Own Research	2	4	2	3
	Friends	2	2	1	2
	Recruiter	1	0	0	2
Sponsorship	Did	1	0	2	2
	Will/May	2	5	0	2
	Did and Will	3	0	0	2
	Didn't and Won't	2	1	1	2
Maintenance of Ties	Parents	8	6	0	3
	Siblings	2	0	1	4
	Other Relatives	5	4	2	6
	Friends	2	4	0	3
	Others	0	1	1	0
Trips Home	Never Been Back	0	0	2	1
	Every 1-2 Years	6	6	1	1
	Every 3-5 Years	2	0	0	4
	Every 6+ Years	0	0	0	2
Total Sample Size		8	6	3	8

who lived abroad previously had gone through a work transfer. The three Filipinas living abroad had also gone for work but all three accepted domestic jobs in the third country and used their residence in the third country to secure non-immigrant (tourist) visas to the U.S.[40]

The structural conditions facing the three Filipinas who came to the U.S. through indirect migration reflect global economic development processes and the institutional involvement of the Philippine government in contractual labor migration as discussed by Tyner (1999). In his article, Tyner stressed the significance of the Philippine government's participation in labor recruitment to the Middle East through formalized agencies such as the Overseas Employment Development Board (OEDB), the National Seaman Board (NSB) and the Bureau of Employment Services (BES)[41] and stressed the fact that such institutionalized recruitment played a relatively minor role in the immigration of Filipinos to the United States.

According to Tyner, the comparatively liberal immigration policies in place in the U.S. in the 1970s and 1980s, the development of a gendered service sector in the U.S. at the same time (e.g., with rising demand for health care workers) and the availability of unskilled labor from Central and South America played much more important roles in the increased migration of professionals from the Philippines than did specialized recruitment. However, Tyner also noted that labor migration to the U.S. occurs through hidden flows (i.e., outside the system of occupational preferences). These three Filipina respondents represent a very important example of the latter.

As discussed in Chapter 4, the 1970s saw the beginning of an increased demand for health care providers, particularly nurses, in the U.S. and a concomitant shortage of trained nurses within the native population. The 1965 Immigration and Nationality Act amendments, along with subsequent laws, encouraged the immigration of Filipina nurses through the occupational preferences. However, the respondents in this research claimed that substantial backlogs for the 3rd and 6th preference visas under the 1965 law hindered movement to the United

---

[40] These respondents specifically cited the extensive backlogs for visas to the U.S. as reasons for their decision to immigrate to some third country.

[41] The Philippine government merged these offices in 1982 to form the Philippines Overseas Employment Administration (POEA).

States[42]. In the absence of a contractual system between the U.S. and the Philippines, these potential respondents faced either years of waiting in the Philippines or use of an alternative path to the U.S. These women chose to utilize the contractual arrangements in place between the Philippines and several East Asian countries as a stepping stone to U.S. migration. After obtaining work contracts as domestics, these trained nurses gained entry to the U.S. through tourist visas and then overstayed the terms of those visas in order to remain in the United States. Eventually, they legalized their status and obtained nursing jobs in the United States.

The patterns of movement exhibited by these three Filipina respondents reflect both the gendered system of migration and the importance of immigration legislation as an institutional control in the immigration process. The demand for nurses, coupled with the gendered notion that care-giving requires feminine traits, encouraged the development of a nursing migration stream to the United States and other developed countries. Finally, Tyner stressed the role that legislation plays in individual migrant decision-making. As shown in Chapter 3, legislative measures significantly affect the availability of ties which, in turn, influence the decisions that individuals make in their own immigration. When faced with an unfavorable legislative environment (i.e., the large occupation-based backlogs) these women found alternative pathways to migration.

However, in most of the cases in this study, legislative conditions did not aid or hinder the respondents either in their decision to migrate or in the actual act of immigration. When asked about the impact of legislative measures, most respondents reported that they simply acted within the confines of the United States' immigration system but that this had little impact on their decision to migrate and did not interfere in any way with their move. Most respondents said they waited no more than a couple of months for visa processing.

The patterns of arrival and adaptation also differed substantially between Indians and Filipinos. Work and educational (non-immigrant) visas predominated among both groups as the original means of immigration into the U.S. However, among Indians, women arriving as dependents of their husbands represented all of the Indian entries in the

---

[42] Two women waited at least four years between the time they sent in their applications in 1969 and the date they were approved for an occupational visa.

"Other" visa category while, in the case of Filipinos, the women who entered originally as tourists accounted for these "Other" entries. The differences between categories of respondents citing other visas reflect another form of gendered migration, this time in the case of Indian immigrants.

As Morokvasic (1984) pointed out, traditional views of the immigration process see women's migration as either an outgrowth of marriage or autonomous female migration. Although viewed as overly simplistic by some accounts, gender-related process can lead to these outcomes. In this study, for instance, Filipina immigrants entered the U.S. primarily as autonomous agents whereas a majority of the Indian women came through marital relations.

Despite the fact that education serves as the primary means of entry for a large number of Indians (Kurien, 1999), this does not hold true in the case of married women. Among my respondents, all of the married Indian women entered as dependents of their husbands. Rangaswamy (1996) reported similar findings in a study of Indian women in Chicago. According to Kurien, Indian gender norms encourage women to sacrifice their own career goals to facilitate their husbands' success in their education and job. In Kurien's research, she found that family migration typically occurred as male-led movement with the husband's search for better professional opportunities. Similarly, despite the high educational backgrounds of the female Indian respondents in this study, most appeared to follow this pattern of female self-sacrifice for husband's success.

The primary reasons cited for coming to the United States included educational opportunities, employment prospects and the presence of family and friends. However, only one of the Filipino respondents cited education as a major consideration in his move. Although several Filipino respondents attended school in the U.S. and obtained degrees here, this occurred primarily as a result of the situation they faced on arrival and the need for further credentials. In a related fashion, most of the Filipino respondents came immediately to the New York area due to familial ties and improved job prospects in the area. Indians, on the other hand, given their greater likelihood to cite education as a motivation, often resided in some other region of the United States for school before moving to the New York metropolitan area.

The next section addresses more fully some of the network features presented in earlier chapters. In the context of the specific research questions cited in an earlier section of this chapter, the following section examines network structure, longitudinal changes in the networks of professionals, the resources upon which professionals rely and the norms influencing immigration decisions of professionals. Although the answers to the questions that follow are based on very small sample sizes the results suggest some important relationships and trends in the immigration process.

What structural forms do immigrant professionals' networks take?

Combining results presented in Tables 5-3 and 5-4 with those in Table 5-5 suggests that immigrant professionals rely heavily on weak tie contacts to employers and educational institutions for immigration to the United States. Seventy-eight percent of the respondents entered the U.S. originally through either a non-immigrant employment visa (i.e., H-1A or H-1B), a student visa (i.e., F1) or as the dependent of an individual with one of these types of visas. However, several caveats to this claim bear mention. First, four of these respondents entered on an employment visa through the sponsorship of an employer with ties to their country of origin. These individuals transferred jobs between the sending country and the United States. Such a transfer cannot be thought of as a pure form of weak tie since some close relationship between the respondent and his/her superior in many cases accounted for the exchange.

A second point relates to the reliance of Indian women on their husband's employment sponsorship for their own immigration. Although their husband's entry may reflect the predominance of weak ties, their own immigration hinges on the strong tie of matrimony. As discussed above, these differences in network usage relate directly to the gender norms prominent in India which place husbands' professional attainment above that of their wives.

Finally, in nearly every case, immigrants reported some reliance on family and friends during their immigration experiences. Most reported some use of close associates for obtaining information on jobs, housing and other resources upon arrival. A majority also cited the influence of family and friends on their decision to migrate in the first place. Most of the respondents knew either family or friends already resident in the United States before arriving, a fact which supports the focus group finding that most of the respondents had some tie to the United States before their decision to immigrate.

The results, therefore, suggest that immigrant professionals take a great deal of personal responsibility for their move but rely on both strong and weak ties to meet their objectives. In most cases, no single type of tie predominates. Rather, individuals take advantage of the opportunities that arise and take assistance from a variety of sources to implement their decisions. In addition, the resources they use originate in both the sending and receiving societies, suggesting that encouragement from family in their home countries plays some role in "pushing" them towards immigration to the United States while the information available from contacts within the U.S. "pulls" them in a similar fashion.

Do professionals utilize enduring social ties or simply "action sets"?
Following up on the previous question suggests that the ties which professionals utilize represent more than just action sets. In Chapter 2, I suggested that migrant networks develop out of networks not necessarily related to the immigration process. The usual conceptions of migrant networks assume migration occurs as part of a family strategy of income diversification and supplementation. This does not appear to hold in the case of professionals. Most of the respondents did cite economic-related factors as part of their reason for moving to the United States and most suggested that family involvement in their immigration decision involved simply encouragement for individual growth and the realization of greater personal opportunities.

These findings of a lack of direct family involvement support newly developing conceptions of the "moral economy" within traditional household migration perspectives (Pessar, 1999). According to this perspective, migration does not necessarily occur as a conscience household strategy for income diversification or supplementation. Family members, and migrants themselves, may consider migration as a means of individual fulfillment with economic and/or social gain accumulating later. This new perspective not only supports the findings reported here but also findings from previous studies such as Hondagneu-Sotelo's (1994) study of undocumented immigrants in which very few people migrated as part of a conscience household strategy.

Despite the fact that most of the respondents in this study reported relatively little reliance on their social connections as an aid in the immigration process, the ties they developed proved important in many ways and usually served longer-term interests. In other words, the maintenance of ties between immigrants and their original employers, co-workers and, certainly, family and friends suggests that the ties operate as something more than simple "action sets." Immigrants may use their contacts to meet specific short-term goals, but the level of continuous interaction suggests greater involvement in the immigration process.

Are there differences in network usage by sex, nativity and occupation?

I presented some evidence with respect to this question in the previous sections of this chapter. Certainly, Indian and Filipino respondents in the sample differ with respect to their circumstances of arrival including date and visa status. However, does this mean that they utilize networks much differently? Among this group of respondents network use does not appear to differ. Most respondents utilized family and friendship contacts during their initial stages of settlement for temporary housing, information on visas and job prospects. However, no systematic differences emerged between the two ethnic groups.

With respect to providing aid to others, Indians and Filipinos appeared almost equally likely to have sponsored someone else to come to the U.S. or at least to feel willing to sponsor someone at a future date. Most reported the same willingness to provide aid to other immigrants, particularly close friends and relatives. Several respondents said that the type of aid they would provide would depend on the person migrating but nearly all said they would share information and related resources.

The initial structural elements of migrant networks of Indians and Filipinos may, therefore, differ but both groups seem to perpetuate similar types of networks over time; occasional direct involvement in the migration processes of others, widespread sharing of information regarding the immigration process to anyone requesting it and significant maintenance of ties between their origin country and the U.S. (85.7% of the Indian respondents travel to India once every one or two years while 54.5% of the Filipinos return to the Philippines at least every five years).

The small sample sizes employed did not permit comparison of differences across occupations within native groups. Some very clear differences arose with respect to the sex of respondents but any effort to disentangle the effects of sex and occupation would require a larger sample size. As noted earlier, Indian male engineers and Filipina nurses represented a majority of the respondents so the sample also did not contain sufficient diversity to explore sex-occupation interactions. In addition, the particularly small sample of Filipino men prevented meaningful comparisons between the sexes for Filipino respondents.

I discussed some differences by sex among Indians earlier. Male respondents came to the U.S. either for employment or educational opportunities while the majority of the women came after marriage or otherwise as dependents of their husbands. As indicated above, these sex differences stem from important gender norms within India which place a higher premium on men's careers than women's. When probed for other reasons for migrating, a couple of the Indian women specifically stated that, although employment prospects would be better for them in the U.S. than in India, their husband's careers took precedence over their own. One Indian woman I interviewed gave up a lucrative career as a professor in a prestigious medical college in India to join her husband in Seattle who found a job with his MBA degree that earned him better pay than she felt she could earn.

One reason for the preference shown towards Indian men's careers within this sample may stem from the fact that most of the men interviewed, and the husbands of the women sampled, obtained their degrees from the best engineering and business schools in India. Women represent extremely small percentages of the students enrolled in these institutions, which likely also reflects some gender bias in the educational training women receive in India. A large percentage of the graduates of these schools take employment abroad due to the inadequate financial returns to employment in India itself. As discussed in the focus group session (the Indian respondent attended one of these premiere institutions), the normative structure of these institutions encourage international migration.

Kurien (ibid.) discussed the fact that Indians generally do not support individual immigration by women for fear of sexual corruption in the United States and other Western countries. The climate fostering immigration at these engineering and science institutions likely interacts with the norms regarding women's immigration to both discourage female enrollment and, in turn, autonomous female immigration.

Do resources play an important role in the immigration process?
Most of the immigrants did not rely so heavily on others for their immigration that without adequate financial support in the United States they would not have come. However, in 36% of the cases, respondents cited access to friends and relatives in the destination area as the primary reason for choosing the initial state of residence. However, this figure includes five Indian women who entered the United States with their husbands, whose acceptance in a particular educational institution or through employment determined their initial area of settlement. Therefore, although the women cited family as the primary reason for settlement, economic considerations actually dictated this choice.

The results from the survey run counter to those in Chapter 4 in the sense that Indians more often chose to settle in areas of greater economic returns (i.e., their job took them there or the school they chose to attend provided them with financial aid) while 36.4% of the Filipinos chose to settle where they did specifically because they had relatives in the area. In the fourth chapter I found that both Indians and Filipinos relied heavily on the presence of fellow-natives in their choice of initial residence in the 1980s but that economic opportunities provided a greater draw to Filipinos arriving in the U.S. in the early 1990s. According to the same set of analyses, Indians retained their reliance on fellow-natives throughout the 1980s and the 1990s. Two of the Filipino respondents citing family as a reason for their choice of location arrived prior to 1990 (one arrived in 1986 while the second came in 1969), which would follow from the Chapter 4 findings, but the other two respondents arrived in the same period as the Indian respondents. These contradictions do not necessarily invalidate the findings here, however, since I limited the analysis in Chapter 4 to particular visa categories.

Do professionals face strong normative pressures to aid family, friends and fellow-natives in further immigration?
The previous chapters could not deal adequately with the question of what role norms play in the immigration of professionals. The survey instrument included several questions to determine how norms affect the immigration process. The questions focused on sponsorship, types of aid provided and the immigrant's own reliance on aid.

The previous sub-section discussed the use of resources among the immigrants sampled. As noted, all of the immigrants made frequent use of contacts already present in the United States (mostly close friends or relatives) to aid them in the settlement process. Few of the respondents reported relying on ethnic associations to assist them in their initial settlement with the exception of those respondents who entered the U.S. to attend school. In all of these cases (all Indian men), the respondents reported using information and aid provided by the Indian association at their school for establishing both temporary and permanent residence, for finding information on community resources, for establishing social contacts and eventually, in some cases, for aid in finding a first job.

Norms pertaining to assistance appeared to affect the sponsorship decisions of the respondents. Seventy-two percent of the respondents had either sponsored a relative to come with them to the United States, had sponsored someone in the years after their arrival or said they thought it likely they would sponsor someone in the future. Among the six respondents who said they had not and would not sponsor anyone, most of these said all of their friends and family already resided in the United States while one individual said he had no close family to sponsor.

The strongest norms, therefore, appear to operate with respect to close ties of the respondent, not unexpectedly. Respondents reserved the most intimate forms of assistance for their friends and relatives. However, almost all of the respondents appeared to feel some sense of duty to others immigrating from their country of origin. One Filipina even said she would be willing to help anyone in any way for the purposes of "survival."

Do the ties of occupational immigrants encourage further immigration?

Occupational ties do appear to lead to further immigration, particularly through sponsorship of relatives as derivative beneficiaries. Most of the Indian men who came to the United States on occupational or educational visas sponsored their wives to join them. Those Indians with permanent resident visas first obtained sponsorship through their employers while those currently holding H-1B visas expected their companies to sponsor them so that they might obtain permanent residence and then sponsor their wives for their own green cards.

Similarly, nearly all of the Filipinos in the sample became citizens of the United States with a majority first obtaining permanent residence through company sponsorship. Several of the Filipino respondents had, however, come in under the 3rd and 6th preference categories of the 1965 Immigration Act Amendments and therefore did not require company sponsorship. These same immigrants, however, sponsored others to join them later.

The most important drawback to the method of interviewing employed relates to the inability to study follow-up migration. Without probes of second- and third-order contacts it is impossible to determine whether those persons sponsored by a spouse, for example, sponsored other relatives. However, some indirect evidence indicates perpetuation of migrant networks among professionals in the case of the Indian women interviewed. Most of these women had been sponsored as dependents of their husbands who, in turn, obtained entry through some form of weak-tie. When asked about their intentions to sponsor others, all replied in the affirmative (although none had actually done so yet since most only recently obtained permanent residence). Future research of a similar nature should examine more extensive network contacts among respondents by interviewing the original migrants, those sponsored by the original migrant, those sponsored by the individuals who were themselves sponsored, and so on.

Comparison with Findings from Similar Studies
The results of this chapter agree with individual aspects of the four studies cited in an earlier section. One of the most consistent findings across all of the research discussed concerned the importance of gender differences in network development and usage. Matthei (1996) addressed the importance of studying gendered processes in migration experiences. She cited evidence that "women play an active role in organizing their own migration" (p. 42) through their participation in already established networks but also through development of same-sex ties. However, she also suggested that this level of involvement occurs more frequently among less-skilled or undocumented entries.

Bashi's (op. cit.) study offered support to Matthei's claims since women represented a majority of the hub householders in her study, the individuals most responsible for offering assistance. Gender differences also arose in Bashi's research with respect to the economic opportunities encountered by men and women once they arrived in the United States. In other words, her data support the idea that women take an active part in migration and network building but that structural conditions in the receiving society affect the efficacy of networks in subsequent stages of immigrant adaptation.

The study of undocumented Mayans in Houston (Hagan, op. cit.) also found gender-based distinctions with respect to patterns of settlement. Women developed networks separate from the men in the sample but in this case the same-sex ties could not overcome the labor market constraints. My results support Matthei's assumption that professional women do not benefit as much from same-sex networks as do less-skilled women and support the traditional notion that these women migrate "as dependents of males or [through tapping] into already established male networks" (Matthei, op. cit., p. 41). However, this appears true only in the case of the Indian women interviewed and does not apply to the Filipinas in the sample. Differences appear to exist across occupations, therefore, since a majority of the Indian women held jobs in male dominated professions (i.e., engineering, medicine and the sciences) while the Filipinas worked in a female-dominated profession (i.e., nursing). Further research should examine these occupational differences and look for more evidence in support of these findings using a larger sample.

These studies also shared a common view of immigration occurring as a multi-faceted process. Both Bashi and Menjivar stressed the importance of examining networks that develop to encourage and assist in movement, and those that aid in socioeconomic adjustment. My results clearly support this view. All of the immigrants I interviewed described their immigration experiences as an array of interconnected processes in which certain types of ties proved more essential than others but which linked together to shape their lives in the U.S. It may be fruitful in future research to map out distinct types of networks among immigrants (i.e., to examine nth-order ties in an individual's job network versus their social network) and to determine whether, and to what extent, they overlap to form a larger migrant network.

The study of norms among immigrant professionals also finds some concurrence with Bashi's study. Bashi found that three types of aid predominated in the networks she studied: legal, housing and job finding. The respondents in my study cited exactly these three types of aid as those they had either provided previously or would be willing to provide at some later stage. In the case of professionals, legal aid usually manifested itself in the provision of advice and information and most of the respondents had not provided any long-term housing assistance on a regular basis (as Bashi had found with some of her hub households). However, my respondents did offer whatever assistance they could in helping other recent immigrants find jobs. Many of these professionals also seemed to feel some sense of responsibility to assist others, offering evidence in favor of Bashi's idea that a "norm of reciprocity" exists among immigrants.

DISCUSSION AND CONCLUSIONS
This phase of the research attempted to fill in some of the gaps in knowledge left by analyses in the previous chapters, as well as to provide a context for understanding the patterns observed. The chapter began with discussion of the results of a focus group survey with five immigrant professionals employed in the New York metropolitan area. I then used the data from this focus group session to help develop a survey instrument for administration to a small non-random sample of professionals employed in the four occupations under consideration. Although the results from both the focus group and the survey interviews do not offer representative perspectives on immigrant networks, they do provide some initial insights among a subset of professionals.

The surveys confirmed earlier findings that substantial differences exist with respect to network structure between sending countries and between the sexes. The small sample sizes precluded any clear statement regarding the extent of differences across occupations, however, since I could not distinguish the effects of sex and occupation. The patterns of entry among Indians and Filipinos appeared consistent with respect to time of arrival and forms of sponsorship as outlined in previous studies.

The results appeared to contradict the finding in Chapter 4 that Filipinos arriving after 1990 relied more heavily on economic resources in the area of destination and that Indians emphasized ethnic communities but this may result from the fact that the analysis in Chapter 4 focused on only two particular modes of entry. Several of the Filipinos who entered after 1990 and who cited family in the area as a primary reason for their initial choice of residence, originally entered the United States on tourist visas.

The data support the view that the networks of professionals incorporate important elements of both strong and weak tie contacts. However, professionals appear far less dependent on either source as a means of entry than occurs with many of the less-skilled populations studied previously. Although professionals make use of their contacts to meet specific goals during the immigration process, the data also suggest that these ties prove more enduring than those implied in the term "action set."

Finally, normative pressures operate to perpetuate migration that originates with strong *and* weak tie admissions. All of the respondents either provided some type of aid to other immigrants or said they would be willing to and almost all either sponsored someone to come to the U.S. at some point or indicated that they would do so at some future date. The data suggest that economic-based admissions *do* perpetuate further migration although the extent to which this occurs could not be determined with the available data.

These topics clearly warrant future survey research. Some suggestions for improvement in study design include the development of a larger sample, greater representativeness of the survey participants, interviews with second-and third-order contacts as typically occurs in social network analysis, and development of a more extensive survey instrument to tease out some of the important relationships not adequately covered in this preliminary study. One great challenge facing any researcher into this topic involves obtaining an adequate sample of all of the professions under consideration. Emphasis must be given to developing techniques to secure the cooperation of physicians and other professionals whose working hours and time commitments leave them feeling too overtaxed to participate in this type of research project or more extensive ethnographic studies.

CHAPTER 6
Findings from the Study of Immigrant Professional Networking

OVERVIEW

This research sought to expand upon the network literature as it pertains to immigrants. Unlike previous studies in this area, the present research attempted to cover a number of sending areas as opposed to focusing on a particular country, to address a previously excluded socioeconomic group (professionals) and to present a more useful and broad-based conceptualization of how networks operate among recent immigrants. The study addressed several specific questions including: 1) What are migrant networks and how do professionals make use of them?; 2) Do differences in network usage exist according to personal characteristics such as occupation, sex and nativity?; 3) What impact do legislative measures have on the availability and use of networks?; 4) Does network usage change over time?; 5) How do networks affect the use of resources? and 6) What role do norms play in the operation of migrant networks?

The study design attempted to incorporate elements of an ethnosurvey in its use of a variety of data sources and research methods. I supplemented quantitative analyses of national level data sets with qualitative techniques, including a focus group session and a personal survey conducted with immigrant professionals. The design falls short of the ideal, however, in its failure to collect relevant information from the sending countries, the lack of sufficient longitudinal data for individual respondents and the inadequate sample sizes employed. With these constraints in mind the study offers some important insights into the process of network formation and use across a sub-sample of professional occupations.

141

MAJOR FINDINGS

Chapter 1

The first chapter outlined previous and current theoretical approaches to the study of immigration, generally, and indicated that networks are now seen as an important component of the immigration process. A review of the literature further suggested that significant gaps in knowledge remain with respect to the migration patterns of professionals. Finally, the chapter outlined the approach to be taken in the analyses to follow.

Chapter 2

In the second chapter I attempted to outline a more general framework for understanding the form and content of migrants' networks. It began with a basic model of networks including the following four primary components: 1) network structure; 2) longitudinal aspects of network development; 3) the role of resources in network use and 4) the role of norms. Based on this general structure, I discussed the fact that a variety of networks exist depending on the configuration of these four elementary factors. In particular, I identified employment-migrant networks and spousal-migrant networks as two specific cases of networks relying on weak and strong ties, respectively.

The importance of this reconfiguration of network construction lies in its applicability to a larger number of immigrant circumstances. Previous studies emphasized the role of strong ties and treated the development of networks as a conscience effort to facilitate immigration. The second chapter attempted to show that weak ties play an important role in network development; as important, in some cases, as strong ties. The discussion further implied that networks might develop out of existing ties which play no role, initially, in the immigration process but become important under circumstances of particular need. Immigration may occur in these cases, not as a conscience family strategy, but as an afterthought in the search for personal fulfillment.

Chapter 3

Chapter 3 focused on two important aspects of migrant networks: network structure and the possibility of changes in networks over time. The longitudinal aspect examined in this phase of the research did not address changes at the individual level. Rather, I emphasized macro-level changes in network availability due to legislative measures put in place in the receiving country. However, these macro-level effects have an important impact on individual network usage among professionals and suggest a shift in emphasis away from strong tie networks towards weak tie networks in the face of legislative decisions, or vice versa.

The results from Chapter 3 suggest that weak ties to potential employers play a very significant role in the immigration process among professional workers. In some years, weak ties clearly predominate over strong ties as a means of entry. The analyses also found that structural conditions in the sending and receiving societies affect individuals differently depending on their sex and occupation. In general then, the study found significant support for the claims that strong ties do not necessarily predominate in the immigration process, that network usage varies depending on individual characteristics and that migrant networks change over time in response to conditions in both the sending and receiving societies.

Chapter 4
The fourth chapter sought to deal with the issue of resources in the immigration process. To this end, I analyzed several types of resources available in the receiving areas and examined the effect those resources had on the settlement patterns of immigrant professionals. I again limited the analysis to macro-level resources since the national data files used do not contain this type of information at the individual level. I further restricted the study to Indians and Filipinos in order to facilitate comparisons and to serve as a bridge to the fifth chapter, which consisted of personal interviews with Indian and Filipino professionals.

The results indicate that the use of resources available in the receiving country differs according to immigrant sex, occupation and nativity. The effects of sex and occupation could not be disentangled entirely, however, so it remained unclear which factor predominated. The findings suggested the possibility of occupational clustering, with engineers and nurses settling in areas with larger concentrations of fellow-natives, although the data provide no way to directly test this hypothesis. Finally, the type of resources predominating appeared to change over time with distinct differences between Indian and Filipino respondents. In the 1980s, both groups of immigrants chose areas with large numbers of fellow-natives. The 1990s saw a continuation of this pattern among Indians but economic conditions in the receiving area became more important predictors of Filipino settlement patterns at that time.

The findings from this chapter have important implications for the study of immigrant networking. They suggest that as a migrant stream becomes more established, some degree of self-perpetuation in the flow of individuals to a destination country leads to the "cumulative causation" of the flow. However, since Indians did not exhibit the same pattern of settlement as Filipinos, the results also suggest that this continuity in migrant streams depends on different factors for different native groups. Further analysis would be required to determine how and why those differences develop.

Chapter 5

The fifth chapter utilized a focus group discussion and individual interviews to explore some of the gaps left in the previous sections of the study. In addition to providing some additional evidence in favor or against the conclusions reached in the previous chapters, Chapter 5 sought to provide the only real evidence regarding the role of norms in the migration process. The national level data sets used in the earlier chapters do not collect information at the individual level, which would offer the necessary conclusive evidence in favor or against the conclusions drawn. However, given the small sample size employed in this phase of the research the results do not lend themselves to definitive conclusions.

Although based on insufficient sample sizes, the characteristics of the survey participants mirror those expected from a larger sample. For example, the Filipinos interviewed had come to the U.S., on average, much earlier than the Indian respondents. The data available from these respondents also seemed to support many of the earlier findings with strong and weak ties both playing important roles in the immigration process for these professionals, differences in network usage between the sexes and extensive use of a variety of resources. However, the results at this stage contradicted those of Chapter 4 in that those Indians arriving in the 1990s responded more clearly to economic considerations in the receiving areas while Filipinos arriving in the same period were influenced more by the location of fellow-natives.

The study also provided some suggestion of answers to long-standing questions in the immigration literature. The weak ties of professionals *do* appear to represent enduring ties utilized at various stages of the migration and adjustment process. Although the data did not explore more extensive network patterns, the results suggest that migration through employers spawns more extensive migrant networks. Finally, norms encourage the furtherance of migrant networks with respect to sponsorship, providing information and other resources to potential immigrants and in maintaining ties between home and destination countries to facilitate information exchange.

Study Limitations

As discussed earlier, although the study design falls short of the ideal, it offers a richer perspective than previous studies based on the use of a variety of data collection methods. In addition to the general problems created through cost and time constraints, several more specific factors limit the study's findings. The first involves the lack of direct information on migrant networks from the Immigration and Naturalization Service's and Census Bureau's data files. Coupled with the inability to obtain a larger sample for the individual interviews, this leaves many of the study's conclusions on questionable ground. Without the requisite individual-level data many of the results remain limited to macro-dimensional circumstances.

Lack of more extensive information on conditions in the sending country also leave many questions unanswered. This study could not, for example, adequately determine how networks develop in the sending country. Many would-be immigrants never make the trip abroad for a variety of reasons including, possibly, the lack of sufficient network resources to undertake the journey. Omitting those individuals in the sending country who never manage to immigrate and without interviewing respondents in the receiving country who somehow fail to meet their goals or obtain positions in line with their qualifications, leaves us with only a limited view of how networks operate to facilitate migration for some but hinder migration for others.

Suggestions for Future Research

This study suggests avenues for future research into the topic of network usage among immigrant professionals. The most obvious starting point for future studies is the development of a comprehensive survey instrument. The survey should include a more representative sample of respondents and a larger number of source countries and occupations. A study currently underway and similar in nature, the New Immigrant Survey (NIS) (Jasso et al., 1997), focuses specifically on new legal immigrants to the United States. An extensive study of that kind will offer improved generalizability of findings and provide important insights on network development over time.

A more expansive survey project should also attempt to analyze higher-order contacts. This study emphasized first-order contacts due to lack of sufficient information and resources. Although I gathered some evidence in favor of the view that professionals utilize and develop extensive migrant networks, without probing more distant contacts it remains impossible to establish the truth to these claims. It also proves impossible to determine the actual extent of networking without some attempt to study the entire network structure. In the language of social network analysis, therefore, this study focused on ego-centered networks but should be expanded to the socio-centric level in order to offer sufficient evidence of network patterns.

The analyses presented suggest two particular areas for future research with respect to the study of immigrant professionals: gender effects in the immigration process and improved research designs to encourage compliance for qualitative analysis. In an attempt to bring gender issues into the study of immigration, many scholars have turned to analyses focused exclusively on women. However, as Tyner (ibid.) noted, researchers need to distinguish between gendered migration and sex-based differences in migration patterns and avoid treating gender studies and studies of women as equivalents. Recent analyses (e.g., see the January issue of *American Behavioral Scientist*) appear more cognizant of these distinctions.

However, a majority of the studies analyzing women's migration and gendered processes in immigration remain focused on less-skilled or undocumented immigrants. Hondagneu-Sotelo (1999) drew attention to the special need for further research into gender patterns of immigration among women professionals in the following statement:

> Significant lacunae remain with respect to what we know about gender in the migration of the many highly educated professional and entrepreneurial immigrants who came to the United States in significant numbers in the 1970s and 1980s (p. 571).

Although I made some attempt to address gender issues at various stages of my study, the data collected for the fifth chapter suggest a need for much more extensive research.

Most research into gendered migration utilizes the ethnographic case study. Such an approach offers tremendous insight into specific sub-populations but does not facilitate reasonable generalizations. In addition, several authors note that the choice of method significantly influences study results (Pessar, 1999; Kurien, 1999). For example, Kurien (ibid.) discussed findings from the two predominant, and conflicting, bodies of literature regarding the effect of gender on Indian women's social standing. The majority of studies found that migration either led to greater empowerment of women and increased gender equality or increased institutionalization of inegalitarian and restrictive models of womanhood. Kurien explained these contradictory conclusions as a function of the choice of method and data sources used.

More extensive and comparative analyses (including comparisons across sending countries and classes) would permit the development of generalized theories of gendered migration patterns but should remain supplemented with case-specific studies. In this way we can attempt to answer questions regarding the development and success of same-sex migrant networks (e.g., Can women in male-dominated fields develop effective same-sex networks and, if not, how will gender processes influence the migration patterns of these women?), the impact of migration on gender relations (e.g., Does migration empower women or undermine their status?) and the source of class differences (e.g., How does globalization affect the supply and demand for labor in prominent receiving countries and how do these effects translate into migratory flows among unskilled and highly skilled workers?). These topics represent a small number of potential areas for future research into the migration of professionals and their use of networks.

A second area for future research applies to the study of professionals using qualitative methods. As found in previous studies,

I discovered that professionals generally feel unwilling to devote sufficient amounts of time for qualitative methods of data collection. Physicians in particular showed extreme reluctance to participate in my research despite assurances of their confidentiality and very limited intrusion on their time. In a recent collection of essays regarding the study of elite populations through qualitative methods Hertz and Imber (1995) summed up the problem succinctly, "Few social researchers study elites because elites are by their very nature difficult to penetrate. Elites establish barriers that set their members apart from the rest of society" (p. vii).

Thomas (1995) suggested employing a variety of techniques in order to gain access to corporate elites. In addition to scheduling contacts during relatively convenient hours (e.g., during the lunch period) and making use of networks established during the research process, Thomas found it best to combine the interviewing methods preferred by targeted respondents (e.g., utilize personal surveys but conduct the interviews by phone), recognizable associations (e.g., personal affiliations with direct interest to the target population) and personal contacts. However, little research offers promising methods for gaining access to elite populations for intensive ethnographic research. Traditional methods, such as participant observation, prove especially difficult to implement among professional groups since the researcher often lacks the necessary credentials to gain access to organizations and meetings.

CONCLUSION

This study offered many important insights into the patterns of network development and usage among immigrant professionals but primarily serves as a source of topics for more extensive future research. In the years to come, immigrant professionals will likely represent a sub-population of increasing relevance to social scientists. Given the greater distance to source countries, the inaccessibility of many sub-groups of professionals for qualitative studies and the current lack of sufficient groundwork, the study of professionals poses special challenges for those studying immigration and its processes. However, as research proceeds, analyses may become more focused and the relevant areas of inquiry more sharply defined.

Appendix

Exhibit 5-1: Focus Group Participant Survey

All responses to the following items and any information you provide during the course of the focus group discussion will be held in strict confidence by the researcher.

Name: _____

2. Occupation: _____

3. Highest Degree Earned (Please also specify the field in which you earned your degree):

_____ in _____

(Degree)   (Field of Study)

4. Country of Birth: _____

5. Primary Country of Residence Between the Ages 0 and 14: _____

6. Year of Initial Entry into the United States: _____

7. Visa Status Upon Entry to the United States: _____

8. Current Visa Status: _____

9. I acknowledge that the purposes of the focus group and subsequent research regarding Immigrant Professionals in the United States were adequately explained to me _____ and I hereby grant my permission for the researcher, Ann D. Bagchi, to use the information I provide for the future development of a survey instrument _____.

Exhibit 5-2: Moderator's Guide

Introductory Remarks:

Thank you for agreeing to participate in this focus group addressing the experiences of highly trained professionals in immigrating to the United States. A focus group can be understood as a directed discussion designed to gather data and information on the topic of interest to the researcher. Often times, data from the focus group are used independently as a means of data collection but in other cases these data are used as the first stage in a broader data collection process. Today's meeting qualifies in the latter category in that the information you provide will be used to develop a formalized survey instrument to study the immigration experiences of professionals employed in the New York Metropolitan Statistical Area. Your participation is entirely voluntary and I personally ensure your confidentiality. Your participation also implies your willingness to comply with maintaining the confidentiality of the other participants. I would like to stress the fact that the focus group is intended as a *discussion* of the topic of interest. There are no right or wrong answers, you may freely discuss the experiences of others you know so long as you do not reveal their names and I encourage you to respectfully share conflicting points of view. If there are no questions I would ask you to fill out the *Focus Group Participant Survey* (intended only to provide demographic characteristics and other relevant information regarding the group's composition - your name will not be used in any way in any subsequent reports). Thank you and now let's begin.

Question Route:
1) Think back to time you were considering emigrating and tell us about your experiences. Specifically, think about the following:
- What were your primary reasons for leaving your country of origin?
- What made you choose the U.S. rather than some other country?
- What were some factors that determined which visa you sought?
- What were your primary sources of information?

2) What are some of the primary obstacles an immigrant faces (either in their attempt to gain entry to the U.S. or, after entering, in adapting to American society) and what resources can one rely on to successfully negotiate these obstacles?

3) What is a personal network?
- Family?
- Friends?
- Employers?
- Fellow Natives?
- Other types of contacts?

4) In what ways and in which situations can immigrants benefit from the use of personal networks?

5) Which types of networks are more useful to professionals in the short term and in the long term?
- Informal ties to family and friends?
- Formal ties to employers, head hunters, etc.?
- Differences in the function of networks depending on the situation?

Exhibit 5-3: Survey Questions

CODE: ENG #   SCI #   PHY #   RN #

DEMOGRAPHIC QUESTIONS:
Personal basic demographic information.
D1. Sex: M   F

D2. What is your birth date? _____

D3a. What is your current marital status? (If never married go to question D4)
    Never Married   Married   Widowed   Divorced   Separated
D3b. Please provide the following information on your current/recent spouse:
    Country of Birth: _____
    Visa Status: _____
    Age: _____
    Educational Attainment: _____
    Occupation: _____

D4. In which country were you born? _____

Educational background.
D5. In which country did you complete your education? _____

D6a. What was the highest degree you attained in your country of birth? _____
(If respondent completed schooling in country of birth skip to Q. D7)
D6b. What is, overall, the highest degree you attained? _____

D7. In which field did you earn your highest degree? _____

LONGITUDINAL MIGRATION HISTORY QUESTIONS:
Number of Trips to the United States

I1a. Did you reside in any countries other than your country of birth prior to immigrating to the United States? Yes / No (No, skip to Q. I2).

I1b. Country: _____

Purpose of stay: _____

Length of stay: _____

Visa status during stay: _____

I2. How many trips to the U.S. did you make before settling here? _____
For each trip obtain the following:

Purpose of stay: _____

Length of stay: _____

Visa status during stay: _____

I3. What was your reason for moving to the United States? _____

I4. In what year did you come to the United States to stay? _____

I5. What was your visa status when you first came to the United States to settle? _____

I6. To which city and state did you first move when you decided to settle in the United States? _____

Current immigrant status.

I7a. Are you now a citizen of the United States? Yes / No
(If yes, obtain the information below then go to Q. S1, otherwise go to Q. I5b)

Date of citizenship: _____

Sponsor: _____

I7b. Are you now a permanent resident of the United States? Yes / No
(If yes, obtain the information below then go to Q. S1, otherwise go to Q. I5c)

Date of permanent residence: _____

Sponsor: _____

I7c. What is your current visa status? _____

STRUCTURE OF NETWORKS QUESTIONS:
Persons/agencies involved in most recent entry to the United States.
S1. Did anyone, (e.g., family, friends, fellow employees or fellow classmates) encourage you to move to the United States? Yes / No
If Yes, obtain the following information:
Individual: _____
Relationship to immigrant: _____
Home or destination country: _____

S2. What were your sources of information, financial and social support during your move abroad (either in home country or in destination country)?
Source of support: _____
Type of support: _____
Home or destination country: _____

RESOURCES OF NETWORKS QUESTIONS:
Resources related to job.
R1. What were the occupational title and job description of the first job you held in the United States? _____

R2. How did you find out about your first job in the United States (e.g., friends, family, employer or co-worker in country of residence, advertisement, Internet, recruitment officer, advisor, "head hunter," etc.)? _____

R3. Do you currently hold the same job as the first job to which you were hired? Yes / No
(If Yes, skip to question R6)

R4. What is your current occupational title and job description?
_____

R5. How did you find out about your current job? _____

Resources related to social relationships.
R6. Do you belong to any associations or clubs? Yes / No
If Yes, obtain the following information:
Name of association/club: _____
Purpose of organization: _____

R6. Do you maintain ties to your country of birth? Yes / No
If Yes, obtain the following information:
How often visit country of birth and who do they visit: _____
People immigrant keeps in touch with:
Person: _____
Means of contact: _____

NORMS REGARDING MIGRATION QUESTIONS:
Sponsorship expectation and practice.
N1. When you decided to settle in the United States, did you sponsor
any relatives to come to the United States with you? Yes / No
If Yes, who did the immigrant sponsor: _____

N2. Do you think you will sponsor anyone to come to the United States
at some time in the future? Yes / No
If Yes, who does the immigrant intend to sponsor:_____

Providing aid to others.
N4. Do you think family, friends or fellow natives will expect you to
provide information and/or assistance at some future date so that they
might immigrate to the United States? Yes / No
If Yes, what type of aid is the immigrant willing to provide: _____

Bibliography

Arnold, Fred, Urmil Minocha and James T. Fawcett. 1987. "The Changing Face of Asian Immigration to the United States." Ch. 6, Pp. 105-152 in *Pacific Bridges: The New Immigration from Asia and the Pacific Islands.* Eds. James T. Fawcett and Benjamin Carino. Staten Island, NY: Center for Migration Studies.

Barringer, Herbert, Robert W. Gardner and Michael J. Levin. 1993. *Asians and Pacific Islanders in the United States.* New York: Russell Sage Foundation.

Bashi, Vilna. 1997. *Survival of the Knitted: The Social Networks of West Indian Immigrants.* Dissertation Abstracts International, A: The Humanities and Social Sciences. 75(12): 5306-A.

Bouvier, Leon F. and David Simcox. 1994. *Foreign Born Professionals in the United States.* April. Washington, D.C.: Center for Immigration Studies.

Boyd, Monica. 1989. *"Family and Personal Networks in International Migration: Recent Developments and New Agendas." International Migration Review.* 23(3): 638-670.

Buroway, Michael. 1976. "The Functions and Reproduction of Migrant Labor: Comparative Material from Southern Africa and the United States." *American Journal of Sociology.* 81(5): 1050-1087.

Carino, Benjamin V. 1996. "Filipino Americans: Many and Varied." Chapter 22, Pp. 293-301 in *Origins and Destinies: Immigration, Race and Ethnicity in America* Eds. Silvia Pedraza and Ruben G. Rumbaut. Belmont: Wadsworth Publishing Company.

Cheng, Lucie. 1984. "The New Asian Immigrants in California." Paper presented at the Conference on Asia-Pacific Immigration to the United States. Honolulu: East-West Population Institute. September 20-25.

Clark, Robert. 1970. "The Asian Subcontinent: The Migration of Talent in Perspective." Pp. 179-214 in *The International Migration of High-Level Manpower: Its Impact on the Development Process.* Committee on the International Migration of Talent. New York: Praeger.

Daniels, Roger. 1993. "United States Policy Towards Asian Immigrants: Contemporary Developments in Historical Perspective." *International Journal.* Spring. 48:310-334.

Davern, Michael. 1997. "Social Networks and Economic Sociology: A Proposed Research Agenda for a More Complete Social Science." *American Journal of Economics and Sociology.* July. 56(3): 287-302.

157

Domrese, Robert J. 1970. "The Migration of Talent from India." Pp. 215-257 in *The International Migration of High-Level Manpower: Its Impact on the Development Process.* Committee on the International Migration of Talent. New York: Praeger.

Espiritu, Yen Le. 1996. "Colonial Oppression, Labour Importation and Group Formation: Filipinos in the United States." *Ethnic and Racial Studies.* January. 19(1): 29-47.

Fawcett, James T. 1989. "Networks, Linkages and Migration Systems." *International Migration Review.* 23(3): 671-680.

Fawcett, James T. and Fred Arnold. 1987a. "Explaining Diversity: Asian and Pacific Immigration Systems." Chapter 19, Pp. 453-478 in *Pacific Bridges: The New Immigration from Asian and the Pacific Islands.* Eds. James T. Fawcett and Benjamin Carino. Staten Island, NY: Center for Migration Studies.

_____. 1987b. "The Role of Surveys in the Study of International Migration: An Appraisal." *International Migration Review.* 21(4): 1523-1540.

Findlay, Allan M. and L. Garrick. 1990. "Scottish Emigration in the 1990s." *Transactions, Institute of British Geographers.* Vol. 15: 177-192.

Findlay, Allan M. and F.L.N. Li. 1998. "A Migration Channels Approach to the Study of Professionals Moving to and from Hong Kong." *International Migration Review.* Fall. 32(3): 682-703.

Findlay, Allan M. et al. 1994. "Doctors Diagnose Their Destinations. *Environment and Planning A.* Vol. 26: 1605-1624.

Fortney, Judith. 1972. "Immigrant Professionals: A Brief Historical Survey." *International Migration Review.* Spring. 6(1): 50-62.

Friedman, S. 1973. "The Effects of the U.S. Immigration Act of 1965 on the Flow of Skilled Immigrants from Less Developed Countries." *World Development.* Vol. 1.

Gardner, Robert W., Bryant Robey and Peter C. Smith. 1985. "Asian Americans: Growth, Change and Diversity." *Population Bulletin.* October. 40(4): 2-43.

Garrick, L. 1991. *A Channels Framework for the Study of Skilled International Migration.* Unpublished Ph. D. thesis, University of Glasgow.

Granovetter, Mark S. 1973. "The Strength of Weak Ties." *American Journal of Sociology.* May. 78(6): 1360-1380.

_____. 1974. *Getting a Job: A Study of Contacts and Careers.* Cambridge, MA: Harvard University Press.

Grieco, Elizabeth M. 1998. "The Effects of Migration on the Establishment of Networks: Caste Disintegration and Reformation Among the Indians of Fiji." *International Migration Review.* Fall. 32(3): 704-736.

Gurak, Douglas T. and Fe Caces. 1992. "Migration Networks and the Shaping of Migration Systems." Chapter 9, Pp. 150-175 in *International Migration Systems: A Global Approach.* Eds. Mary Kritz, Lin Lim and Hania Zlotnick. Oxford: Clarendon Press.

Hagan, Jacqueline. 1998. "Social Networks, Gender and Immigrant Incorporation: Resources and Constraints." *American Sociological Review.* February. Vol. 63(55-67).

Hertz, Rosanna and Jonathan B. Imber, eds. 1995. *Studying Elites Using Qualitative Methods.* Thousand Oaks, CA: Sage Publications.

Hondagneu-Sotelo, Pierrette. 1994. *Gendered Transitions: Mexican Experiences of Immigration.* Berkeley, CA: University of California Press.

_____. 1999. "Introduction: Gender and Contemporary U.S. Immigration." *American Behavioral Scientist.* January. 42(4): 565-576.

Hwang, Sean-Shong, Rogelio Saenz and Benigno Aguirre. 1995. "The SES Selectivity of Interracially Married Asians." *International Migration Review.* 29(2): 469-491.

Ishi, Tomoji. 1987. "Class Conflict, the State and Linkage: The International Migration of Nurses from the Philippines." *Berkeley Journal of Sociology: A Critical Review.* 32: 281-312.

Jasso, Guillermina, Douglas S. Massey, Mark R. Rosenzweig and James P. Smith. 1997. "The New Immigrant Survey (NIS) Pilot Study: Preliminary Results." Paper presented at the Population Association of America Annual Meeting. Chicago.

Kanjanapan, Wilawan. 1995. "The Immigration or Asian Professionals to the United States, 1988-1990." *International Migration Review.* 29(1): 7-32.

Keely, Charles B. 1971. "Effects of the Immigration Act of 1965 on Selected Population Characteristics of Immigrants to the United States." *Demography.* May. 8(2): 157-191.

Knodel, John. 1997. "A Case for Nonanthropological Qualitative Methods for Demographers." *Population and Development Review.* December. 23(4): 847-853.

Krueger, Richard A. 1988. *Focus Groups: A Practical Guide for Applied Research.* Newbury Park: Sage Publications.

Kurien, Prema. 1999. "Gendered Ethnicity: Creating a Hindu Indian Identity in the United States." *American Behavioral Scientist.* January. 42(4): 648-670.

Lee, Sharon M. 1993. "Racial Classifications in the United States Census: 1890-1990." *Ethnic and Racial Studies.* 16(1): 75-94.

Light, Ivan, Parminder Bhachu and Stavros Krageorgis. 1993. "Migration Networks and Immigrant Entrepreneurship." Chapter 2, Pp. 25-49 in *Immigrants and Entrepreneurship: Culture, Capital and Ethnic Networks.* Eds. Ivan Light and Parminder Bhachu. New Brunswick: Transaction Publications.

Lindquist, Bruce. 1993. "Migration Networks: A Case Study of the Philippines." *Asian and Pacific Migration Journal.* 2(1): 75-104.

Liu, John M. 1992. "The Contours of Asian Professional, Technical and Kindred Work Immigration, 1965-1988." *Sociological Perspectives.* 35(4): 673-704.

Liu, John M., Paul M. Ong and Carolyn Rosenstein. 1991. "Dual Chain Migration: Post-1965 Filipino Immigration to the United States." *International Migration Review.* 25(3): 487-513.

Lobo, Arun Peter and Joseph J. Salvo. 1998. "Changing U.S. Immigration Law and the Occupational Selectivity of Asian Immigrants." *International Migration Review.* Fall. 32(3): 737-760.

Louis, K.S. 1982. "Multisite/Multimethod Studies: An Introduction." *American Behavioral Scientist.* 26:6-22.

Madigan, Francis and Imelda Pagtolun-an 1990. "The Philippines." Chapter 16. Pp. 287-300 in *Handbook on International Migration.* Eds. William Serow, Charles Nam, David Sly and Robert Weller. New York: Greenwood Press.

Massey, Douglas S. 1987. "The Ethnosurvey in Theory and Practice." *International Migration Review.* 21(4): 1498-1522.

_____. 1988. "Economic Development and International Migration in Comparative Perspective." *Population and Development Review.* September 14(3): 383-413.

_____. 1990. "Social Structure, Household Strategies and the Cumulative Causation of Migration." *Population Index.* Spring. 56(1): 3-26.

_____. 1996. "The Age of Extremes: Concentrated Affluence and Poverty in the Twenty-First Century." *Demography.* November. 33(4): 395-412.

Massey, Douglas S., Joaquin Arango, Graeme Hugo, Ali Kouaouci, Adela Pellegrino and J. Edward Taylor. 1993. "Theories of International Migration: A Review and Appraisal." *Population and Development Review.* September. 19(3): 431-466.

Massey, Douglas S., Rafael Alarcon, Jorge Durand and Humberto Gonzalez. 1987. *Return to Aztlan: The Social Process of International Migration from Western Mexico.* Berkeley: University of California Press.

_____. 1994. "An Evaluation of International Migration Theory: The North American Case." *Population and Development Review.* December. 20(4): 699-752.

Matthei, Linda Miller. 1996. "Gender and International Labor Migration: A Network Approach." *Social Justice.* 23(3): 38-53.

Melendy, H. Brett. 1977. *Asians in America: Filipinos, Koreans and East Indians.* Boston: Twayne Publishers.

Menjivar, Cecilia. 1997. "Immigrant Kinship Networks and the Impact of the Receiving Context: Salvadorans in San Francisco in the Early 1990s." *Social Problems.* February. 44(1): 104-123.

Minocha, Urmil. 1987. "South Asian Immigrants: Trends and Impacts on the Sending and Receiving Societies." Ch. 15, Pp. 347-373 in *Pacific Bridges: The New Immigration from Asia and the Pacific Islands.* Eds. James T. Fawcett and Benjamin Carino. Staten Island, NY: Center for Migration Studies.

Mitchell, J. Clyde. 1969. "The Concept and Use of Social Networks." Chapter 1, Pp. 1-50 in *Social Networks in Urban Situations: Analyses of Personal Relationships in Central African Towns.* Ed. J. Clyde Mitchell. Manchester: Manchester University Press.

Morawska, Ewa. 1990. "The Sociology and Historiography of Immigration." Chapter 7, Pp. 187-238 in *Immigration Reconsidered: History, Sociology and Politics.* Ed. Virginia Yans-McLaughlin. New York: Oxford University Press.

Morgan, David L. 1996. "Focus Groups." *Annual Review of Sociology.* Vol. 22: 129-52.

Morokvasic, Mirjana. 1984. "Birds of Passage are Also Women..." *International Migration Review.* 18(4): 886-907.

Myers, Raymond H. 1990. *Classical and Modern Regression with Applications, 2nd Edition.* Boston: PWS-Kent Publishing Company.

Neter, John, William Wasserman and G.A. Whitmore. 1993. *Applied Statistics, 4th Edition.* Boston: Allyn and Bacon.

Neuman, W. Lawrence. 1997. *Social Research Methods: Qualitative and Quantitative Approaches, 3rd Edition.* Boston: Allyn and Bacon.

Ong, Paul and Tania Azores. 1994. "The Migration and Incorporation of
    Filipino Nurses." Chapter 6, Pp. 164-195 in *The New Asian Immigration
    In Los Angeles and Global Restructuring*. Eds. Paul Ong, Edna Bonacich
    and Lucie Cheng. Philadelphia: Temple University Press.

Ong, Paul M., Lucie Cheng and Leslie Evans. 1992. "Migration of Highly
    Educated Asians and Global Dynamics." *Asian and Pacific Migration
    Journal*. 1(3-4): 543-567.

Papademetriou, Demetrios G. and Stephen Yale-Loehr. 1996. *Balancing
    Interests: Rethinking U.S. Selection of Skilled Immigrants*. Washington,
    D.C.: Carnegie Endowment for International Peace.

Passell, Jeffrey S. and Rebecca L. Clark. 1998. *Immigrants in New York: Their
    Legal Status, Incomes and Taxes*. April. Washington, D.C.: The Urban
    Institute.

Pessar, Patricia R. 1999. "Engendering Migration Studies: The Case of New
    Immigrants in the United States." *American Behavioral Scientist*. January.
    42(4): 577-600.

Piore, Michael. 1979. *Birds of Passage: Migrant Labor and Industrial
    Societies*. Cambridge: Cambridge University Press.

Portes, Alejandro. 1987. "One Field, Many Views: Competing Theories of
    International Migration." Ch. 3, Pp. 53-70 in *Pacific Bridges: The New
    Immigration from Asia and the Pacific Islands*. Eds. James T. Fawcett and
    Benjamin Carino. Staten Island, NY: Center for Migration Studies.

Rangaswamy, P.I. 1996. *The Imperatives of Choice and Change: Post 1965
    Immigrants From India in Metropolitan Chicago*. Unpublished doctoral
    dissertation. Department of History. University of Illinois, Chicago.

Reimers, David. 1983. "An Unintended Reform: The 1965 Immigration Act
    and Their World Immigration to the United States." *Journal of American
    Ethnic History*. Fall. Pp. 9-28.

Ruth, Heather Low. 1970. "Philippines." Pp. 46-80 in *The International
    Migration of High-Level Manpower: Its Impact on the Development
    Process*. Committee on the International Migration of Talent. New York:
    Praeger.

Sassen, Saskia. 1988. *The Mobility of Labor and Capital: A Study in
    International Investment and Labor Flow*. Cambridge: Cambridge
    University Press.

Scott, John. 1991. *Social Network Analysis: A Handbook*. Thousand Oaks:
    SAGE Publications.

Singh, Gurdial. 1945. "East Indians in the United States." *Sociology and Social
    Research*. Vol. 30: 208-216.

Smith, Peter. 1976. "The Social Demography of Filipino Migrations Abroad."
    International Migration Review. Fall. 10(3): 307-353.

Stark, Oded. 1991. *The Migration of Labor.* Cambridge, MA: Basil Blackwell.

Taylor, J. Edward. 1986. "Differential Migration, Networks, Information and
    Risk." Pp. 147-171 in *Research in Human Capital and Development:
    Migration, Human Capital and Development.* Eds. Oded Stark and Ismail
    Sirageldin. Greenwich: JAI Press, Inc.

_____. 1987. "Undocumented Mexico-U.S. Migration and the Returns to
    Households in Rural Mexico." *American Journal of Agricultural
    Economics.* Vol. 69: 616-638.

Thomas, Robert J. 1995. "Interviewing Important People in Big Companies."
    Chapter 1, Pp. 3-17 in *Studying Elites Using Qualitative Methods.*
    Rosanna Hertz and Jonathan B. Imber, eds. Thousand Oaks: Sage
    Publications.

Todaro, Michael. 1976. *International Migration in Developing Countries: A
    Review of Theory, Evidence, Methodology and Research Priorities.*
    Geneva: International Labour Office.

Tomasi, S. and Charles Keely. 1975. *Whom Have we Welcomed? The
    Adequacy and Quality of United States Immigration Data for Policy
    Analysis and Evaluation.* New York: Center for Migration Studies.

Tyner, James A. 1999. "The Global Context of Gendered Labor Migration
    From the Philippines to the United States." *American Behavioral Scientist.*
    January. 42(4): 671-689.

U.S. Bureau of the Census. 1972-1992. *Statistical Abstract of the United States.*
    Washington, D.C.

_____. 1983. *Census of Population and Housing, 1980: Public Use
    Microdata Sample A* [machine readable data file] / prepared by the Bureau
    of the Census. Washington, D.C.: The Bureau.

_____. 1992. *Census of Population and Housing, 1990: Public-Use
    Microdata Samples U.S.* [machine readable data files] / prepared by the
    Bureau of the Census. Washington, D.C.: The Bureau.

U.S. Department of Justice. Immigration and Naturalization Service. 1972-
    1992. *Immigrants Admitted to the United States.*

U.S. Immigration and Naturalization Service. 1953-1977. *Annual Report of the
    Immigration and Naturalization Service.* U.S. Government Printing
    Office: Washington, D.C.

_____. 1978-1995. *Statistical Yearbook of the Immigration and
    Naturalization Service.* U.S. Government Printing Office: Washington,
    D.C.

Vasegh-Daneshvary, Nasser, Henry W. Herzog, Jr. and Alan M. Schlottmann. 1986. "College Educated Immigrants in the American Labor Force: A Study of Locational Behavior." *Southern Economic Journal.* January. Vol. 52: 818-31.

Waldorf, B. 1996. "The Internal Dynamic of International Migration Systems" *Environment and Planning, A.* Vol. 28: 631-650.

Wallerstein, Immanuel. 1974. *The Modern World-System.* New York: Academic Press.

Wellman, Barry and S.D. Berkowitz. 1988. "Introduction: Studying Social Structures." Chapter 1, Pp. 1-18 in *Social Structures: A Network Approach.* Eds. Barry Wellman and S.D. Berkowitz. Cambridge: Cambridge University Press.

Westoff, Charles and Robert Parke, Jr., Eds. 1972. "Immigration into the United States with Special Reference to Professional and Technical Workers." *Demographic and Social Aspects of Population Growth, Vol. 1.* The Commission of Population Growth and the American Future Research Reports.

Yochum, Gilbert and Vinod Agarwal. 1988. "Permanent Labor Certifications for Alien Professionals, 1975-1982." *International Migration Review.* 22(2): 265-281.

Zeitlin, Maurice. 1974. "Corporate Ownership and Control: The Large Corporation and Capitalist Class." *American Journal of Sociology*, 79(5): 1073-1119.

Index

Printed in the United States
3366